THE SIPSTER'S POCKET GUIDE
TO 50 MUST-TRY BC WINES

VOLUME 2

VOL.

2

THE

SIPSTER'S

POCKET GUIDE
TO 50 MUST-TRY
BC WINES

LUKE WHITTALL

TOUCHWOOD

Cover and interior design by Sydney Barnes
Photographs by Luke Whittall

CATALOGUING DATA AVAILABLE FROM LIBRARY AND ARCHIVES CANADA
ISBN 9781771513944 (softcover)
ISBN 9781771513951 (electronic)

TouchWood Editions acknowledges that the land on which we live and work is within the traditional territories of the Lkwungen (Esquimalt and Songhees), Malahat, Pacheedaht, Scia'new, T'Sou-ke and W̱SÁNEĆ (Pauquachin, Tsartlip, Tsawout, Tseycum) peoples.

We acknowledge the financial support of the Government of Canada through the Canada Book Fund and of the Province of British Columbia through the Book Publishing Tax Credit.

This book was produced using FSC®-certified, acid-free papers, processed chlorine free, and printed with soya-based inks.

Printed in China

27 26 25 24 23   1 2 3 4 5

For John Schreiner,
my mentor in this amazing world of BC wine who has,
to my knowledge, never had a wine book dedicated to him.

sipster

sip·ster | \ sip-stər \

: one who observes, seeks, and sets taste trends of sipping beverages, such as wine, spirits, tea, and coffee, outside of the mainstream.

CONTENTS

INTRODUCTION

CELEBRATING THINGS THAT MATTER

Welcome to Volume 2 of *The Sipster's Pocket Guide*. The unofficial subtitle of this volume should be "What a difference a pandemic makes!" Sipsters are always aware and appreciative of the things that they eat and drink, but in the post-pandemic world, I believe that appreciation is much more widespread. When social gatherings, large or small, are taken away, it makes us appreciate them even more once they're possible again. Wine is a social product, and those who work in the industry are often highly social people. Even though I never really liked the crowded nature of the huge, noisy tastings at the Okanagan Wine Festivals or the Vancouver International Wine Festival, I really missed them when they were absent.

Our attitudes toward wine, especially local wines, and local food have also shifted noticeably since before the pandemic. If you saw wine as a luxury indulgence before Covid, it likely became more of a necessity during the worst of the lockdowns. When we were isolated in our homes, alcohol was rightly considered as essential as toilet paper and bread. Just as grocery stores remained open, so did liquor stores. People placed orders for wine online, perhaps for the first time, and had it shipped or picked it up curbside. Maybe they joined a wine club or two. Companies purchased virtual tastings for their employees, and many people gathered for tastings on video calls with friends. It was a busy time for the wine industry online.

The first volume of *Sipster's* was conceived, written, and published during the pandemic. I hoped that reading about wine would also be deemed essential for those missing the in-person tastings and the experiences that normally come with the wine lifestyle. The aromas and flavours of a special wine can transport us back to memories of the "Before Times." It is my hope that all of these experiences, coupled with a new-found appreciation for the essential elements that wine can bring to our lives, will help us to get further past the "point scores and tasting notes" approach to learning about wine: *Did someone give that wine only 86 points? I had that wine with my parents during our last visit, and we all thought it was fantastic. I guess those points don't mean very much after all.*

Covid also brought a real fear to many who work in the wine industry, particularly the possible symptom of losing one's sense of smell. Losing, or even compromising, that sense is a serious threat to the professional lives of those working with wine. It can seriously impede a winemaker from doing their job for weeks. It can be a safety risk to cellar staff, who have no way to detect a developing fault in a barrel or, say, a propane leak from the forklift. Even those in wine sales can have great difficulties doing their work with their olfactory senses compromised (for example, not being able to detect a faulted bottle). Hopefully more research into this aspect of the virus will take place in the near future. Perhaps it will help us understand more about this generally undervalued sense.

OUR RELATIONSHIP WITH ALCOHOL

Following the first set of pandemic lockdowns, many people began re-examining their relationship with wine and with alcohol in general. As Edward Slingerland notes frequently in his fantastic book *Drunk*, drinking alone can be dangerous. Unless your partner is a bartender, there's probably nobody serving you drinks or, more importantly, monitoring how much you're drinking when you're working from home. As we all know, "self-monitoring" means something entirely different from being aware of how many glasses of wine you've had in an evening. Slingerland suggests that societal pressures and obligations often act as a kind of safeguard against overconsumption of alcohol. In cultures where wine is treated like a food and enjoyed only with meals, alcohol abuse in general is reduced. When those societal pressures are removed due to isolation at home, what are our safeguards?

For some people, societal pressures (or encouragement) come from social media, which can be a lifeline for human interaction and information (although that is certainly debatable). In the past, organized religion had a hand in guiding morals; social media has taken on that role today. Slingerland notes that "our age is moralistic to a degree not seen since Queen Victoria's day."* It is difficult to discuss topics constructively with the binary "I'm right" and "You're wrong" of social media platforms. Shades of meaning go out the browser window and arguments tend to become all or nothing. Just like in Victorian times, you are either a good person or you are branded as a witch. There is no in between. Similarly, at one time you were allowed to consume alcohol, or you weren't. This moralism resulted in the total prohibition of alcohol in BC and the rest of North America just over a century ago.

Being self-aware of our consumption habits, personally and as a society, should never be belittled or ignored. I have close friends who have given up drinking altogether, and I will always support them in this. The trend toward no- or low-alcohol wines illustrates a positive corrective measure to the laissez-faire attitudes toward wine depicted in many memes and bedazzled wine-shop T-shirts over the past decade. Sipsters enjoy wine more for what it is than what it does. It is the act of enjoying that is the appeal. Having too much seriously impacts our ability to enjoy wine, which is ultimately just a food and, for some, an important part of life. Pairing wine with food is the best way for sipsters to take the time to appreciate the nuances of wine, the skill that it takes to make it, and the places it comes from.

For sipsters, wine is a journey that's all about the senses, the mind, and the time spent with friends.

*p. 289

THE SIPSTER'S APPROACH

If you read Volume 1, you probably noticed that *Sipster's* takes a unique approach to wine write-ups. The book is a two-way conversation about wine in book form, not a book of wine reviews. I don't proffer my opinion about a wine and then pronounce my score based on the years of experience or accreditations that I have. It is me writing about my experiences with wines that I hope you will enjoy as much as I have. It's as simple as that.

To be clear, I am not trying to sell any of the wines in this book. That is the wineries' job. My job is to provide you with something interesting to read that encourages you to appreciate and enjoy your wines in new ways or reaffirms the way that you have been doing it all along but may never have seen represented in wine media before. Lately, "traditional" wine media (magazines, radio shows) have devolved into advertorials—paid "articles" that accompany advertisements. On the surface, these articles seem like real journalism. But it's a pay-to-play situation, and every question and phrase has likely been closely vetted in advance by the winery. This is not entirely a bad thing* so long as it is above board. There is a big difference between reading a wine enthusiast's genuine opinion about a wine and reading an opinion that the winery *wants* you to read because it fits their message.

Wine bloggers and podcasters filled the void left by this devolution of traditional and critical wine media in Canada. At first, blog writers seemed able to provide a little more subjectivity in their reviews, which was refreshing. Everyone was coming from a place and point of view, which made reading blogs a bit of a wild ride. But it's hard for anyone to turn down free admission to special tastings or free wine in the mail, and this can quickly compromise subjectivity. Bloggers and online "influencers" now must disclose any content that is a paid sponsorship or endorsement. This has made it a lot easier to see when a YouTube video has been sponsored, but it also makes

---

*Full disclosure: I wrote for one of these magazines for seven years. It was a great training ground for a fledgling wine writer, and I am thankful for that experience and the many people that I met along the way.

it more annoying to watch when a beautiful sailing video is interrupted mid-snorkelling scene to discuss the benefits of a body hair trimmer.

For the purposes of transparency, I will tell you that roughly half of the wines tasted for this volume were generously contributed by the wineries when I requested them. The other half were wines that I purchased myself or tasted somewhere like a wine-shop tasting or a friend's house. Contributed or purchased, there was no guarantee that any of the wine I tried would be included in this volume. I continued to write only about wines that I felt were worthy of inclusion.

Perhaps my ideology is difficult for wineries to understand in a time when marketing is all-important. A lot of marketing and wine media (traditional or newer online writing) is based around the notion "You don't know anything about wine and I do. Let me help you understand it." To be sure, wine can be complicated, and most of us jump at anything that will help us impress our new partner, our future in-laws, or our coworkers at the next office party. But, like Apple in the 1990s, there is only so far a company can go when it treats its customers like idiots. That attitude almost sank Apple until Steve Jobs came back to rescue them with his new iThings.

Marketing should still be important, but perhaps we have swung too far in recent years. In the 1990s, most wineries considered marketing unimportant. Hearing the stories in any wine shop or a quick glance through *The Okanagan Wine Tour Guide* will show you that most wineries were started by people who came from other industries. Ninety-nine percent of them were not from marketing backgrounds. Marketing wasn't important then, and BC wine desperately needed it. To paraphrase the late industry pioneer Harry McWatters: What good is it if nobody knows about it? At that time, he was a real rebel. However, there has to be balance. When a wine's marketing is more important than how it was made, something gets lost. These days it seems we have too much marketing and not enough reality.

Right now, there is a lot of good wine being made in BC. Prior to 2010, a book like this would have been impossible to write. There are still badly (or perhaps inexpertly) made wines out there, but they won't appear in this book. I don't have time to write about wines that aren't well made, and I won't waste your time by asking you to read about them. If a wine is included in *Sipster's*, it's a solid, well-made wine. These are all wines that I think you should seek out and experience if what I have written about them appeals to you. At the very least, I hope that you'll be entertained reading about them.

KNOWING WHAT TO KNOW

Sipsters trust their palates. Only they know what tastes good to them, and even if you do not consider yourself a sipster, you can do the same. Nobody else can tell you what to taste, but they can influence you, which is what marketers and wine salespeople try to do. In this second volume, I slightly altered my approach when it came to tasting wines from wineries that were totally new to me. It's an approach that I've borrowed from my partner, who does not like to know anything about a book that she's considering reading. Other than the author and the title, she wants to know nothing about it and will not even read the back cover. Author's bio? No. Reviews? Not a chance. If I even mention the ISBN, she will exclaim, "Hey! No spoilers!"

I tried to adapt this same approach with new-to-me wineries. I don't want to know anything about the winery in advance. I may want to know its approximate location, but that's all. I tune out the story of the winery, the people, and the description of the wine itself until I have tasted it. I want to approach it all through the lens of the wine first.

What we know about a wine in advance can really impact how we perceive it. One serious influencer is the price. As the industry saying goes, "The price is the spice." If we believe that the wine is more valuable, we may be less likely to perceive its abstractions or nuances as faults. Conversely, if we believe a wine to be cheap, we may be more likely to blame those same abstractions or faults on the fact that it's just a cheap bottle of wine. There are quite a few wines from new wineries appearing in this volume as well as ones I have been familiar with for many years. With each one, I tried hard to maintain as much of an open mind as possible by learning as little as possible about each wine before tasting it. In a world dominated by social media and advertorial "pay-to-play" wine media, it wasn't easy to do. It still feels good to be surprised now and again.

A NOTE ON HOW THE WINES WERE TASTED

Just like in Volume 1, all of these wines were enjoyed with food and using various wineglass styles. These ranged from high-quality stemware to the thick-rimmed wineglasses my daughter gave me for Christmas, and even (gasp) stemless wineglasses. Essentially, I used just about any kind of glass that was designed for drinking *wine*. No mugs, tumblers, or juice cups were used.

I did follow some protocols to give each wine the greatest chance to taste its best. Wines were served at their proper serving temperature. White wines were chilled; reds were not. All wines were paired with a suitable food and occasion, and my impressions of the wines were written down immediately, usually with some wine still in my glass.

HOW THE WINES ARE PRESENTED

WINERY AND WINE NAME

WINERY PRICE: ♟ = < $10
♟ ♟ = $10–20
♟ ♟ ♟ = $20–30
♟ ♟ ♟ ♟ = $30–40
♟ ♟ ♟ ♟ ♟ = $40–50

BODY: LIGHT/MEDIUM/FULL
SWEETNESS: DRY/OFF-DRY/MEDIUM/SWEET/LUSCIOUS
ATTITUDE: THE WINE'S PERSONALITY

Pair with: Foods, moods, and occasions

WINERY PRICE: This is the approximate price range of the wine, pretax, as listed on the winery's website. Prices are subject to change at the whim of the winery, of course, so none of the prices listed here are set in stone. They will give you a general sense of what you can expect to pay.

BODY: When wine people talk about the body of a wine, they are referring to the perceived fullness or texture of the wine. I like to describe it in terms of milk. Skim milk feels light and watery. Move up to 2% milk and the texture feels a bit fuller. Homogenized milk will be even fuller, and 10% cream even more so. Wine can be the same way—watery and thin or thick and full. It has nothing to do with the intensity of the flavour, only the sensation of the texture.

Why does this matter? It matters because it affects what you pair the wine with—foods or occasions. The weight of the wine needs to match the weight of the food and the occasion. Hosting a reception outside at your Okanagan wedding in July? A big-bodied red wine probably won't be what you're looking for because in the hot sun nobody will want to drink it. It probably won't work with that cedar-planked salmon on the grill either.

SWEETNESS: During my years in wine sales, I found this was usually one of the first three questions that customers asked me (along with "What are the grape varieties?" and "How much is it?"). It is also one of the most misunderstood factors, so let me try to clear this up. *Dry* means "no sugar." *Off-dry* means that there is a little bit of sugar and to some people, it might taste a little sweet. I've actually had a person taste a late-harvest dessert wine—a wine that is legally mandated to taste sweet—and say, "Oh, that's quite dry."

All I do is nod and silently quote a line from *The Princess Bride* in my head: "You keep using that word. I do not think it means what you think it means."

Winemakers need to be aware of a wine's sweetness because sugar and acidity have to be balanced. Think of it like lemon juice. If you squeeze a lemon to make lemon juice, what do you need to make it drinkable? Sugar! Sugar is what balances the high acidity of the lemon juice, and voila—a refreshing beverage on a hot summer day. If there isn't enough sugar, it will taste sour. Too much sugar and it tastes cloying. Getting that balance right is the key.

Wines in BC, especially white wines, naturally have more acid in them compared to other, hotter wine-growing regions, so a little residual sugar can make a wine balanced. Just like lemon juice, a little bit of sugar balances the wine. The vast majority of red wines in BC are fermented completely dry (no sugar at all).

If the winemaker has done a good job, most people won't even notice that there is sugar in the wine. It will simply taste like a well-made, smooth wine. Sugar is not bad or good. It is there for balance. We've had a couple of generations of wine lovers who grew up thinking that they were not supposed to like sweet wines. If you are concerned about getting head-aches from sweeter wines, consider drinking less in an evening. Problem solved.

ATTITUDE: This is where my wine descriptions really start to diverge from the norm. The characteristics mentioned so far are based on more measurable factors, with body being the description of texture and sweetness being an assessment of sugar that can be accurately measured through laboratory analysis.

Aroma descriptors are not nearly as measurable, and writers must rely on similes to get the point across. One could say that a wine "smells like" black currants, dried mangoes, or tennis balls, but that doesn't mean that the wine actually has those aromas deliberately built into it (though if you are new to wine, I can see how easy that is to assume). It is also one person's perception of that wine, someone who we assume is adequate-ly qualified to make those assessments. Were they trained as a winemaker, a sommelier, or an educator? With the Court of Master Sommeliers? International Sommelier Guild? Wine & Spirit Education Trust? To what level? Does that even matter?

Training inconsistencies aside, the use of only aromatic

descriptors to describe a wine is limited when wines can be described using other linguistic devices. Aromatic similes can go only so far, but images and metaphors can help us understand the wine more deeply. Opening it up gives us a whole new range of instruments to communicate a wine's personality. Lots of wines have "aromas of strawberries and dried herbs," but only this one can be described as being "like a relaxing breakfast with waffles and fresh berries." Some wines are hidden or coy, while others are bombastic or vivacious. Wines are not just wines; they can be like people. They can have attitudes and personalities. The ultimate wine pairing is when the right wine is matched to the right situation.

PAIR WITH: Wines are almost always paired with foods, although even this is historically a relatively recent concept in wine appreciation. Suggestions for food pairings are common in the marketing material provided by wineries, as well as in the banter spouted by eager wine-shop sales staff. There are many books and college courses dedicated to the concepts surrounding pairing. Learning the techniques is a great way to increase your enjoyment of wine at meals.

But what if you don't happen to have duck confit and cherry gastrique prepared for dinner tonight and just want to enjoy a wine on its own? What if you want to have a glass while watching the sun set? What about the best wine for a relaxing bath or maybe a picnic? Matching wine to food is important, but matching it to the occasion should enhance the enjoyment of both more effectively, and more deeply. At its most basic, a truly great pairing is when the two things mutually reinforce each other without one overshadowing the other. The wine should make the food taste better, and the food should make the wine taste better. The same goes for the occasion: the wine should help make it that much more memorable.

In this book I list possibilities for foods, occasions, and moods that I believe will pair beautifully with these wines. You can also use the index at the back and search through the pairing list to find the perfect wine.

Happy sipping!

SPARKLING WINES

Here we go again with the fizz at the front! Starting a meal or a special event with a bottle of bubble brings out the smiles in everyone. It's like we, as humans, have learned that the pop of a sparkling wine being opened is the official shotgun start to whatever fun is about to happen.

"Paging Doctor Pavlov. Please report to the wine cellar."

It is good to celebrate things when we can. I would argue that the pandemic has helped us appreciate the good things we have in life. I would also argue that corralling sparkling wine into the pen allocated only for special occasions means we miss out on many wonderful pairing experiences. Ever had sparkling wine with beef? No? That's a shame. How about with popcorn?

Sparkling wine is in fact *wine* and can be properly matched with any food or occasion, just like any other category of wine. It doesn't have to be a special occasion, nor does it have to be the only bottle of the night. Try a multi-course meal accompanied *only* by sparkling wines. Or reverse the traditional pairing sequence and pour the sparkling wine last with dessert instead of first. Can it be done? Of course! Wine invites us to try new pairings, occasions, and moods.

That is what makes a life of wine so interesting. Cheers to that!

And it has
no alcohol!

BENJAMIN BRIDGE PIQUETTE ZERO

WINERY PRICE: 🍷
BODY: LIGHT
SWEETNESS: OFF-DRY
ATTITUDE: CAREFREE

Pair with: Canoe rides, picnics, and then driving anywhere else afterwards

Okay, whoa! This is clearly not a wine in the technical sense. It is a piquette-style beverage made by a winery in Nova Scotia. And it has no alcohol!

Bear with me for a second.

No wineries in BC are yet producing this style, but it will happen. This piquette should be the new benchmark for this style.

There are few beverages that can do what wine does when you sip it. A good wine has complex aromas and flavours that can change and evolve in the glass right in front of you. Juices, sodas, or flavoured sparkling waters can't do that. You don't have to smell your orange juice to appreciate its flavour. It tastes like oranges. What a shock. Teas, coffees, and other fermented or distilled beverages can offer up complexity, but do they evolve over time? Is that tea really going to be more fantastic if you swirl it and let it sit for a half-hour before tasting it again? Aromatic complexity may be important for these beverages, but there isn't a broad culture of appreciation surrounding them like there is for wine. Non-alcoholic wines have had this same problem. They've been boring to sip. Nobody has been able to make one that is all that interesting.

Until now. Piquette Zero is extraordinary because it can be appreciated in the same way that wine is. Zesty fruit, wild herbs, little white flowers—you can smell a complex array of aromas and sense flavours in it *just like a real wine*. And you'll get something new with every whiff. How does it do that? It has no alcohol but somehow is totally worth your attention.

Sip, savour, and enjoy with abandon.

Did you make it all the way to Wednesday?

ENRICO WINERY CÉLÉBRATION CHARME DE L'ILE

WINERY PRICE: 🍷 🍷 🍷
BODY: LIGHT
SWEETNESS: DRY
ATTITUDE: MERRY

Pair with: Prosciutto, appetizers, celebrating small victories

There is something special about small victories. Learning that your old boss got in trouble for the way they treated you when you worked there years ago. Finding out that you were right all along about someone even though everyone told you there was nothing to be concerned about. Finding a $5 bill at the bus stop with nobody around. In the grand scheme of things, they don't seem like much, but they do mean something.

They can add up too. In those moments, it's nice to have something to celebrate with that isn't over the top but more special than basic import fizz. Not that you have to wait to celebrate something to open a sparkling wine. Anything that is worth something to you is worth celebrating. Did you finish that project? Yay! Time to celebrate. Get the kids to all of their weekend activities? Yay! Time to celebrate. Did you make it *all the way* to Wednesday? Yay! Time to celebrate.

Enter Enrico's Célébration, a Charmat-method sparkler* that looks way more expensive than it is and will have you convinced you are drinking something that should cost a lot more. It has some beautiful bubbly action going on within its golden hue, which perfectly matches the amazing gold-leaf design on the bottle. If Prosecco is your thing, this is the BC equivalent from our own version of Italy, namely Vancouver Island. Now you can celebrate those small victories and buy local as well.

*The name *Charme de l'Ile* was coined by winemaker Daniel Cosman and indicates a Charmat-method sparkling wine made using only grapes from Vancouver Island (the *de l'Ile* part). Other wineries on Vancouver Island and the Gulf Islands are also using that name on their sparkling wines.

It's okay. This wine knows that you won't stray.

HESTER CREEK TI AMO

WINERY PRICE: 🍷 🍷 🍷
BODY: MEDIUM
SWEETNESS: OFF-DRY
ATTITUDE: PLAYFUL

Pair with: Spicy canapés, Cajun catfish, stargazing from the pool deck

---

Yes, obviously the name of this wine suggests love, but this is a playful love. This Prosecco-style sparkling wine is entirely loving in the sense that you will enjoy every sip without arousing any insecurity. Want to have a quick peek at that cute Cava on the shelf? No problem. Did you get caught taking a lustful look up and down at the glamourous grower's Champagne on the menu? It's okay. This wine knows that you won't stray.

Its aromas and flavours will keep you intrigued for hours. No conversation could ever be diluted by sipping this beautiful, easy-drinking sparkling wine. Though it's not a totally dry wine (there is a little residual sugar there), it's not enough to pose problems for the morning after, so enjoy your flirtatious evening and all of the oxytocin-inducing attention that it provides. Even though you may move on to a bigger red wine for the next course, you most certainly won't be searching for another sparkling after you are done sipping this one.

And even if you do, you'll probably still be thinking of the Ti Amo the whole time.

A little more
bounce on the
office stapler.

MOCOJO OH!

WINERY PRICE: 🍷 🍷 🍷
BODY: MEDIUM
SWEETNESS: OFF-DRY
ATTITUDE: RELAXED

Pair with: Spinach salad, Brie, boat trips

It's the last day of work before a long weekend! This makes for a little more spring in the step, a little more bounce on the office stapler, or maybe a little more weight to the foot on the gas pedal. There is an energy to being on the precipice of extra time off that doesn't happen before a normal weekend.

This wine captures that carefree feeling. It has that same energy, that same drive to relax.

Long weekends can mean different things to different people. If you work "regular" hours during the week, the long weekend is time to get out and do what you want to do which, if you want to do nothing, means doing nothing with style. Long weekends are the grand time-out when you can tune out and relax.

The balance between work and life is still a new concept for some people. Where it used to be taken for granted that everyone had weekends off at the same time, these days weekends can be spread out over different combinations of days. For people in the hospitality industry who must work on the weekends and holidays, long weekends can often happen in the middle of the week. Bringing balance to work and life is still important regardless of when you actually get time off.

Whenever the long weekend is for you, this wine is your ticket to the big relaxy.

The aromas from these grapes are clearly in love with each other.

NICHE WINE CO. SMALL BATCH BUBBLES

WINERY PRICE: 🍷 🍷 🍷
BODY: LIGHT
SWEETNESS: DRY(ISH)
ATTITUDE: LOVING

Pair with: Spicy noodles, curries, take-out dinner for two

This wine hits your nose and your palate with a lot of things at once. Though Niche doesn't specify which grapes are in it, the aromas from these grapes are clearly in love with each other. They work well together and complement beautiful cheeses but can also give each other space when they need it. It's a fantastic little dance that happens when you sip between bites.

This means that this wine will have lots of opportunities to tell you that it loves you. And it will work with lots of different things, from special occasions to casual nights in. Spicy take-out? No problem. Pizza with whatever toppings you like? Check that too. Meeting the future in-laws for the first time? You're covered, and you will probably impress their socks off too.

How does a wine do this?

Well, if it was easy, then every winery would be able to do it. But they don't. If you find one that does, then it's truly the right wine for you.

Then, one day,
they go to a
friend's house.

SUMMERHILL PYRAMID WINERY CIPES BLANC DE NOIRS

WINERY PRICE: 🍷 🍷 🍷 🍷 🍷
BODY: MEDIUM
SWEETNESS: DRY
ATTITUDE: HIGH PERFORMANCE

Pair with: Chorizo, paella, making dinner at a friend's place

This wine is finely tuned. The machinery of its flavours is precisely aligned, and it's amazing to see it working in such a unified and seamless fashion. Is it worth the extra money?

Sometimes quality doesn't become noticeable until you try something better. Kitchen knives are a great example. Most people just want a knife that can cut through things with relative ease and reasonable safety. They wonder why anyone would bother paying $400 for a chef's knife when they can get a whole set of eight at a big-box store for $50. They are convinced that nobody should need to pay that much for a knife and will happily go about their lives using their $50 set.

Then, one day, they go to a friend's house. The friend has a high-quality knife set that cost a lot more than $50 for one knife. They can't believe how easy it is to use, how balanced it feels, and how much easier it makes cutting through tomatoes or green peppers. The next day, they try to use their old knives, but something has changed. Their knives don't seem to cut very well anymore. They seem dull, heavy, and almost clunky. Like trying to use a spoon to cut through a tomato. Then they remember how easy it was using the more expensive knives.

Maybe there is something to those high-quality knives after all?

It won't cleanse
your palate so much
as order out any
flavours that are still
hanging around.

Venturi Schulze

2013

BRUT NATUREL

VENTURI SCHULZE BRUT NATUREL

WINERY PRICE: 🍷 🍷 🍷 🍷
BODY: LIGHT
SWEETNESS: DRY
ATTITUDE: DRILL SERGEANT

Pair with: Porchetta, charcuterie, winter hot-tubbing

When I first learned about wine, I was told that wine acted as a palate cleanser. Its simplest task was to rid your mouth of the flavours of the food that you were enjoying so that you could re-enjoy it all over again. I learned that some wines did this better than others and that some types of wine did a better job with specific foods. That was the beginning of a huge learning process about food and wine pairing that continues to this day.

While most wines go about their task cleansing your palate, this sparkling wine is more like a bootcamp drill sergeant. It won't cleanse your palate so much as order out any flavours that are still hanging around. There is no question as to who is the authority. Flavours lounging lazily in your mouth will quickly realize that they have important duties to perform elsewhere. They will leave the mess hall as fast as they can.

Yes, this wine has a pushy edge, but it also means that it can punch above its weight class with food pairings, giving you lots of options. Porchetta? No problem! Salmon with hollandaise sauce? Does this wine look scared to you? Seafood linguini? Do I have "light-bodied" on my label?!

Now drop and give me twenty sips.

WHITE WINES

If the diversity of white wines in this section doesn't convince you that whites are just as thrilling a taste adventure as reds, then I don't know what will. There is such a range of experiences waiting for you with white wines that sometimes it's hard to choose just one. More than any other style, they remind me, in a very literal way, of the beautiful scents and aromas that one experiences while living in wine country.

The complexity of the aromas evolves throughout the season as various fruiting plants flower, ripen, and are harvested throughout the valley. This begins with cherries and then moves through the soft tree fruits like apricots, peaches, and plums, then pears and apples. The growing season comes to a climax with the grape harvest throughout most of the fall. Fields of peppers, tomatoes, and other ground veggies provide the spice that adds complexity to the environment. Normally this kind of thing can only be appreciated by living in wine country full time rather than through the occasional weekend fling. But touring wine country more in the off-seasons will give you the sense that white wines in BC really do mirror the seasons.

It takes Route 3 and stops at every fruit stand and scenic lookout along the way.

CHRONOS

RIESLING

OKANAGAN VALLEY BC VQA

CHRONOS RIESLING

WINERY PRICE: 🍷 🍷 🍷
BODY: MEDIUM
SWEETNESS: DRY(ISH)
ATTITUDE: PATIENT

Pair with: Slow food, slow-roasted pork, long afternoons reading a book

If patience is a virtue (and not a fault, as I recall feeling in university), then this wine is clearly the most virtuous. This wine doesn't scream along the Coquihalla at 130 kilometres an hour (that *is* the speed limit, right?). It takes Route 3 and stops at every fruit stand and scenic lookout along the way. The views are there to be taken in and rushing is not what this wine is about.

There is something decidedly uncool about that attitude today. We want to rush from point A to point B with the same instantaneity as clicking on the next YouTube video. This wine does not go fast and does not care one bit if others do. Go ahead, rush around to get where you need to go. This wine will get there. Eventually.

While most other trendy Rieslings in BC take the fast lane with big petrol and intense acids, Chronos Riesling is sitting in the flower garden, smelling the herbs in the next plot. Yes, there is acid too, but it's not pushy or up front. You will still have all of the enamel left on your teeth after sipping this slowly on a warm spring or fall day.

In a world where everything is telling us to go faster, it's fantastic to find a wine that calmly says, "Hey. Enjoy the moment."

Is it dangerous? Is it good? Is it tasty? What's that sound?

CROWN & THIEVES
WINEMAKER'S WENCH

WINERY PRICE: 🍷 🍷 🍷
BODY: LIGHT
SWEETNESS: DRY
ATTITUDE: EXOTIC

Pair with: Canapés, seafood pasta salads, accompanying yourself on the ukulele

Travelling to new places means that your brain is going to be bombarded with all kinds of new sensory information. When we are in familiar places, such as our homes, workplaces, or travelling between them, our brains tune out the things that we've sensed hundreds of times before. It takes a lot less energy to be in a familiar place because our brains don't need to work as hard to apprehend our surroundings.

Going to a new place gives us stimulation and introduces novelty to our brains. We sense new things, some that are completely foreign to us and maybe others that we've sensed before. Our brains have to work a little harder. We can't assume that our senses have picked up on all of the things that they can. Everything is mysterious. Is it dangerous? Is it good? Is it tasty? What's that sound?

This wine gives that same sense of the exotic that comes from travelling. The novelty that makes travelling addictive for people who love (and feel the deep need to) travel is evident in the aromas of this wine. It's not quite like other whites and is immediately inviting. That same desire for novelty drives sipsters to seek out new adventures with unexplored wines.

Finding this one shouldn't be hard, but it will be satisfying.

The sun goes down
and then that's it,
right? Well, no.

DA SILVA
Vineyards and Winery

CHENIN BLANC
OKANAGAN VALLEY
HIDDEN HOLLOW VINEYARD
2020
13.1% alc./vol, WHITE WINE / VIN BLANC 750mL

DA SILVA VINEYARDS AND WINERY CHENIN BLANC

WINERY PRICE: ♥ ♥ ♥ ♥
BODY: LIGHT
SWEETNESS: DRY
ATTITUDE: PEACEFUL

Pair with: Medium cheeses like Edam or Gouda, chicken Caesar salads, sunsets in English Bay, Tofino, or Kelowna

This wine is a sunset in a glass. At the end of a fantastic day of doing whatever you do, the sunset is your reward. Taking the time to pause and watch the natural light fade from the sky and settle beyond the horizon is a very peaceful way to centre yourself after the tumult of the day.

You might think that sunsets are the same everywhere. The sun goes down and then that's it, right? Well, no. Watching the sun set over the water in Vancouver's English Bay is very different from the long twilight hours in the Okanagan. In places where there are no mountains, the sun can shine straight across the landscape showing all kinds of textures, shadows, and colours. Every sunset spot is enjoyable in its own way.

Sometimes, if we've been living in the same place for a long time, we might not appreciate sunsets as much as we used to. We see them so often that, unless there is a weird cloud formation in the sky, they don't register as being all that special. Even if you have seen a sunset so often at home that it becomes commonplace, this Chenin Blanc will refresh that. It is a palate cleanser for your sunset taste buds, reminding you that your sunset is as beautiful as a vacation spot that you've never been to before.

Sipster's Tip: Pour this wine as cold as you can. That way, as you sip, your tasting experience will change subtly as the wine warms.

The truth is,
I miss you.

HILLSIDE MUSCAT OTTONEL

WINERY PRICE: 🍷 🍷 🍷
BODY: LIGHT
SWEETNESS: OFF-DRY
ATTITUDE: AMOROUS

Pair with: Chocolate, berry-laced desserts, long-distance relationships

Dear Muscat Ottonel,

I know it's been a while since I've written to you. But I also haven't heard back from you in some time. The more time that goes by, the more I miss you and your beautiful aromas. It is hard to believe that we haven't communicated at all in years. Where has all of that time gone?

You should know that I was reminded of you on many occasions over the years. I found an empty bottle of your 2015 vintage at a friend's house once. I've also walked past many vintages at a store I frequent, until recently when I found the shelf you were on empty. Eventually one of the staff came by, removed your price tag, and unceremoniously shuffled the neighbouring wines over to fill in the space.

The truth is, I miss you. There just isn't another grape variety like you out there in BC. Sure, there are other aromatic wines, but they just aren't you. Some are just too flowery, too spicy, or way too acidic. But you are just that perfect balance of fresh fruit and sunshine that makes every day feel a little brighter. Thank you.

Yours always,

Sipster

It has to be
different to feel a
little more special.

HAND-CRAFTED MEAD

HONEYMOON
mead
ODE TO ODIN

375 ML 16% ALC. / VOL. MED. DRY (2)

HONEYMOON MEADERY ODE TO ODIN

WINERY PRICE: 🍷 🍷 🍷
BODY: MEDIUM
SWEETNESS: OFF-DRY
ATTITUDE: CEREMONIAL

Pair with: Hard cheeses, chips and salty snacks, stargazing

Commemorating something—a place, a person, a time—is important. Perhaps with the decreased influence of religious traditions in our society (at least on a widespread scale), marking occasions with ceremonies or rituals is not as common in our daily lives. The big ones are still there, such as weddings, funerals, graduations, and holidays like Christmas, Thanksgiving, and maybe Easter. Beyond that, we seem to have lost the smaller ones somewhere along the way.

Take Sunday dinners. Larger families might still do this sporadically, but it is not as common as it used to be and more reserved for special occasions when the family can get together. Because of this, food that is made for Sunday dinners needs to be special and not just something that could be served on any old day. Canned soup, burgers, or pizza don't really count as special-occasion food. It has to be different to feel a little more special.

Being different is exactly what this is. It's not a wine; it's mead, which is the only serious rival to wine as the oldest crafted beverage. For sipsters on the lookout for something different, opening a bottle of mead is a great way to make the occasion special and make it more commemorative. This mead in particular will stand up to lots of different foods but also be a great experience on its own. It's not a lightweight.

For a beverage that is so old, there are few modern pairing suggestions or accepted traditions for enjoying mead. This leaves it wide open to the possibility of starting something new.

Smart and a little rebellious at the same time.

KETTLE VALLEY PINOT GRIS

WINERY PRICE: ♟ ♟ ♟
BODY: LIGHT
SWEETNESS: DRY
ATTITUDE: REBELLIOUS

Pair with: Cream sauces, ham, puzzle marathons

This wine is like a Rubik's cube solution that has been tattooed on your arm. Smart and a little rebellious at the same time.

The Rubik's cube, the famous but irritating little puzzle that some people learn to master very quickly, is a toy that people either enjoy or enjoy tossing against a brick wall. There is little in the way of ambivalent opinion on it. You would never hear someone say, "Yeah, Rubik's cubes are okay."

Where some wines are made with sledgehammers or belt sanders, this Pinot Gris has been constructed precisely using a CNC machine that can cut out the most intricate parts with extremely fine detail. Its food pairings are accurately measured movements of acidity and flavour. This is a high-wire wine. If the pairing is right, you will have a mind-altering experience. If the pairing is off, solving the puzzle will be more of a challenge.

The reward for solving it makes it totally worth it.

WHITE

What this grape
can do when you
leave it alone and
just let it be.

LITTLE FARM WINERY

MULBERRY TREE VINEYARD · SIMILKAMEEN VALLEY

CHARDONNAY

– 2018 –

LITTLE FARM CHARDONNAY

WINERY PRICE: 🍷 🍷 🍷
BODY: MEDIUM
SWEETNESS: DRY
ATTITUDE: PASTORAL

Pair with: Cheddar, cedar-planked pork tenderloin, fresh-caught fish cooked over a campfire

This winery's name includes a word that may have fallen out of fashion lately. One of those words that's almost offensive to wine people of a certain generation, who have almost stringently objected to its use so much that they refuse to have anything to do with it at all when they go on wine tastings.

That word, of course, is *little*.

Wine lovers seem to be constantly on the hunt for *big*—the big wines and the big flavours. This wine is not actually little in any way, but it's also not big in the way that one might expect with Chardonnay. The flavours are pure without being too crazy or unpredictable. It is balanced the way a well-made wine should be. Chardonnay responds well to almost any winemaking technique like oak aging, malolactic fermentation, or lees stirring (among others). A lot of Chardonnays are made with a lot of different techniques. Little Farm's Chardonnay seems to use few if any of these techniques, which really speaks to what this grape can do when you leave it alone and just let it be.

True, not everyone has been thrilled with Chardonnays lately, but one secret that sipsters know about BC is that Chardonnay can do things here that it can't in other parts of the world. There is a vibrancy to it that is balanced with an aggressive (some might say, too aggressive) set of flavours that push it over the top at times. But it pairs beautifully with Pacific Northwest cuisine which only reinforces the food pairing mantra, "What grows together goes together."

We got out "old" Legos when we were thirteen and talked about memories of the good old days playing with them when we were eight.

MISSION HILL FIVE VINEYARDS PINOT BLANC

WINERY PRICE: 🍷 🍷
BODY: LIGHT
SWEETNESS: DRY
ATTITUDE: COMMEMORATIVE

Pair with: Shellfish, salads, reminiscing

WHITE

Sensory events have power over our brains. We can instantly remember things when we are exposed to similar sights, sounds, or smells and be transported back to when those events were happening. It can inspire a real sense of nostalgia, particularly if the memories triggered are good ones. There are still songs that can instantly bring me back to when I was in high school. Watching old TV shows can be pretty nostalgic as well. Perhaps it's a personality trait. I vividly remember getting nostalgic with my friend Mark as we got out "old" Legos when we were thirteen and talked about memories of the good old days playing with them when we were eight. It was a weird feeling at the time, but I vividly recall how it made me feel.

For whatever reason, this wine always brings me back to 2003 when I first visited Mission Hill. It was really early in the season. There was sod freshly laid down in the amphitheatre and plywood covering the wet concrete walkways. The trees were not very big, and it seemed that everything about the place was brand new. That was twenty years ago now and yet just getting a whiff of the aromas of this wine brings me back.

Moments like that can make one appreciate the things that are more present. Certainly, in the scope of Mission Hill's vast production, this humble Pinot Blanc doesn't command the respect or attention of other wines in their portfolio. It is the polar opposite of their Oculus (the expensive flagship red). Yet, here it is, all these years later, still a part of their portfolio and with a Reserve version available too.

What does it remind you of?

Or at least, that's
what I've been led
to believe.

steen down so long

MODEST WINES STEEN DOWN SO LONG

WINERY PRICE: 🍷🍷🍷
BODY: LIGHT
SWEETNESS: DRY
ATTITUDE: CHEEKY

Pair with: Poached salmon with lemon dill sauce, BBQ *chicken, puns*

WHITE

Humour is not universal. For every person who laughs at a good pun, there are two who groan, and one person who laughs inside and thinks that they could have done it better. What everyone agrees on is that the person who made the pun is clearly the smartest friend in their group.

Or at least, that's what I've been led to believe as a fan of the genre. To wit, the name of this wine is a pun that gives us a clue as to the grape variety that was used to make it. *No Spoilers!* If you need to find out, you'll have to visit Mount Boucherie (the winery that makes and sells Modest Wines to accompany their fantastic restaurant on site) or ask the most experienced sipster in your group.

What is more universal is the appeal of this wine because it has everything for the white wine drinker. The Pinot Gris crowd will find it round enough while the Riesling peeps will love its acidity. Even the ABCers will get in the game with it since there is not a trace of oak to be found. The value for this and other wines in the Modest Wines portfolio, which are indeed modestly priced, will also be universally praised.

Look for it when you are wine Touraine this Saumur.

A little history
in BC and almost
zero respect from
wine lovers.

NAGGING DOUBT SIEGERREBE

WINERY PRICE: 🍷 🍷
BODY: MEDIUM
SWEETNESS: OFF-DRY
ATTITUDE: PAISLEY

Pair with: Butter chicken, Vichyssoise, watching races at Area 27

This wine is liquid paisley. It has curves. Lots of them. It is a perceptibly paisley pattern on the palate, which makes it fantastic to experience. Not a lot of wines can do that. It accomplishes this with a dizzying array of aromas and flavours that are all wrapped up with an appropriately silky texture. The are no harsh flavours and no acidic edges, just curved lines in every direction.

Siegerrebe has a little history in BC and almost zero respect from wine lovers. Sipsters who are well travelled within BC know that it is one of the only grape varieties grown in almost all of the the province's regions. This makes it a really fascinating grape to use to compare wines from many different regions. Unfortunately, it suffers from the same unpronounceability issue that has plagued wines made with grapes like Ehrenfelser or Grüner-Veltliner or places like Pouilly-Fuissé or the Willamette Valley (it's Will-A-mit, dammit). BC is a special place for wines like this. And if Gewurztraminer can do it (becoming the most popular white wine produced in BC for many years), then Siegerrebe can do it too.

Go team Siegerrebe!

If it was possible to earn a merit badge for Chardonnay, this is the wine that would do it.

NK'MIP QʷAM QʷMT CHARDONNAY

WINERY PRICE: 🍷 🍷 🍷 🍷
BODY: MEDIUM
SWEETNESS: DRY
ATTITUDE: SPIRITUAL

Pair with: Smoked salmon, lobster, your favourite blanket

I once found a box of badges somewhere in amongst the things that I had put away a long time ago. It was at a time in my life when things had not been going well and I was teaching myself to sew them onto a blanket I had bought. Some of the badges could be ironed in place, but others had to be sewed on tediously one by one. Slowly over the months, I literally and metaphorically stitched my life back together. When I had used up all of my badges I started looking for new ones from places I visited and wherever I could find them. Online stores provided me with a few more interesting ones, and I have been adding to the blanket casually ever since.

All of these badges mean something to me and some of them had to be earned, just like merit badges in Scouts as a kid. There are badges from the provinces and states where I have lived, countries that are significant to my family history, and places that I've visited. There are badges from schools I've attended and even some movie references.

If it was possible to earn a merit badge for Chardonnay, this is the wine that would do it. Appreciating it will help you understand more about what an amazing variety it can be when grown in the Okanagan. In a blind tasting once, an esteemed winemaker whom I deeply respect said they believed that this wine was from a specific winery in California where they used to work and was totally shocked when the truth was revealed. For full-bodied, age-worthy, south Okanagan Chardonnay, it really doesn't get any better than this.

WHITE

The adventure
of taking wine
where no wine
has gone before.

RECLINE RIDGE WINE 2 GO WHITE

WINERY PRICE: 🍷
BODY: LIGHT
SWEETNESS: OFF-DRY
ATTITUDE: TRAILBLAZING

Pair with: Munchies, hotdogs, off-grid living

Sipsters appreciate tradition, but new things don't bother them. If you enjoy the sound of the cork being pulled on a bottle of wine, that's great. It is a beautiful sound and a pleasure to hear because we expect something good to happen soon after: we're going to taste wine. Synthetic corks came out and still had the same sound, but it was different. Then screwcaps became more common, and that's when the walls went up. Traditional wine folk just said no.

Suffice it to say that if you were bothered by screwcaps, the more recent wine-in-a-can thing isn't going to do it for you either. Which is too bad because you will be missing out on some well-made wines, including this one, which is one of the best wines I've tasted from a can. This wine will do anything you need it to. It's versatile without being bland, which is a hard balance to achieve.

You will also be missing out on the adventure of taking wine where no wine has gone before, be it hiking trips, canoe adventures, motorcycle trips, or even #vanlife. In all of those activities, the weight of your cargo and the durability of the container is probably significant to you. Packing bottles might be okay for some occasions, but cans are lightweight and this 355 millilitre can is larger than most other canned wines. Bring along two of these and you're just shy of a full bottle by volume and packing out the empties is a whole lot easier.

And if you still think you need to hear it, just have someone imitate the cork-pulling sound when you open it.

Just looking at the
bottle will tell you
that this Riesling is
different.

SCOUT RIESLING

WINERY PRICE: 🍷 🍷 🍷 🍷
BODY: MEDIUM
SWEETNESS: DRY
ATTITUDE: SHY

Pair with: Aged Havarti, pork tenderloin with pear glaze, calm days

---

This Riesling is not a wild party. It requires some calm to appreciate it. Just looking at the bottle will tell you that this Riesling is different. If you pick up the bottle and move it around, it may appear a little cloudy. Move it too much and it will cloud over. Let it settle for a day or two in the fridge, and it will reveal a wonderful but still tentative clarity. Be gentle with it as you pour.

A boat trip would not be the ideal place to enjoy this wine. That's not to say that it is too intellectual or obtuse for most wine lovers to enjoy because it is amazingly approachable for a wine of this style. For that relaxing dinner for two or maybe four, this could be your pre-dinner sip while watching food cook slowly on the grill.

Wines made from Riesling can sometimes be a bit unpredictable. Is it going to be sweet? Dry? Tart? Light and crisp? Reading the labels carefully can give you clues about some of those things but not all. What will be revealed when the bottle is opened? Take your time with this one as it reveals itself slowly

Sipster's Tip: Decant this wine. Yes, you can decant a white wine. It will really help reveal this wine's full potential in a most amazing way. Serve only slightly chilled.

You would not shout it out, but you would probably use a loud whisper.

ST. HUBERTUS CHASSELAS

WINERY PRICE: 🍷 🍷
BODY: LIGHT
SWEETNESS: DRY
ATTITUDE: QUIET FORCEFULNESS

Pair with: Fondue, light salads, one-on-one conversations

This wine is like a forceful whisper. It doesn't shout the flavours at you so much as whisper them urgently to your palate as you sip. It's a light-bodied wine, but there are a lot of aromas and flavours there trying to get your attention. With that much acidity (and a little residual sugar to balance it), it won't have trouble succeeding. It will make you pay attention from the very first sip.

In his book *Reading Between the Wines*, American wine importer Terry Theise describes some wines like this. On a podcast interview prior to the book's release, he suggested a scenario that involved people in a movie theatre. If someone behind you is making noise during the movie, you may want to turn around and say, "Would you please be quiet?" Of course, being a thoughtful person, you would not shout it out, but you would probably use a loud whisper.

Though this is not a new wine by any stretch, it is shocking how few people know about it, which may make it the longest-produced legitimate Sipster white wine in BC. If you did know about it, your Sipster credibility is secure. Whisper more about it at your next dinner party.

As if the world were
a much more open
and accessible place.

SUMMERGATE KERNER

WINERY PRICE: 🍷 🍷 🍷
BODY: MEDIUM
SWEETNESS: OFF-DRY
ATTITUDE: SPRIGHTLY

Pair with: Prosciutto, spicy Thai food, frolicking

Walking outside in the cold winter can be energizing, but it can take a lot out of you too, especially if you have to walk far, against the wind, uphill, in two metres of snow (or in Vancouver, in three centimetres of snow). The extra layers of clothing, which can restrict movement, don't help either, and the bulky footwear makes for heavy trodding.

In contrast, going for a walk or hike in the spring is a wonderful feeling. Less clothing gives one a feeling of freedom, as if the world were a much more open and accessible place. Walking is less taxing and more enjoyable. The air is far more breathable, and the scents of thawed earth and budding plants make for a diverse olfactory environment.

This Kerner is very much like a first walk in the spring. There are all of those springtime aromas coupled to a wine that is easy on the palate and never taxing to enjoy. It's a medium wine that gives the impression of lightness and freedom. There are no bulky oak aromas or silky textures to add insulation and restrict your movements. There are only the fresh sensations of spring rejuvenation to make you want to run (or frolic, perhaps?) outside in the warm weather and clean air.

WHITE

Planting the garden
boxes for another
season, getting the
camping gear out
of storage.

TALL TALE WINES

2018
Grüner Veltliner

TALL TALE WINES GRÜNER VELTLINER

WINERY PRICE: 🍷 🍷
BODY: MEDIUM
SWEETNESS: DRY
ATTITUDE: ANTICIPATORY

Pair with: Schnitzel, chicken sandwiches with apples and pears, enjoying sunshine

Each season has a different smell. They are subtle but they are there. They inspire a sense of anticipation for what is to come. Fall smells like dried leaves tinged with a compost-like aroma that anticipates the approaching cold weather. When it does get cold, the air starts to smell like winter, even before the snow starts to fly, with that light frosty smell. When things warm up, spring has a definite aromatic profile that can be little musty, perhaps a little green, and often a bit earthy.

In the Okanagan, the aromas of fall are a relief from the heat while winter's aromas are a warning of things to come (time to put on the snow tires). Spring is different. It's a relaxing feeling knowing that things that were asleep are now reawakening. Grass that wasn't growing will start to grow. Leaves that weren't there over the winter will slowly push their way out.

This wine is late springtime in a glass, complete with those green budding aromas that happen when the leaves finally push out on the trees. It will remind you of the satisfaction of planting the garden boxes for another season, getting the camping gear out of storage, or cleaning off the deck for that first dinner outside.

This wine will make you anticipate all of that and be perfect for celebrating it when it comes.

There is a genuine
desire to help spread
the word and show
others the same joy.

TANTALUS VINEYARDS RIESLING

WINERY PRICE: 🍷 🍷 🍷
BODY: MEDIUM
SWEETNESS: OFF-DRY
ATTITUDE: MENTORING

Pair with: Spicy Asian cuisine, smoked sausages, sipster parties

The concept of mentorship is something that seems to be slipping away from us. Mentors can steer your entire life in a direction that you didn't even know you needed to go. The value of that guidance is massively important. Those of us who have been lucky to have had a mentor at some point in our lives are probably better for it.

Becoming a mentor to someone is equally fulfilling. Watching someone progress and thrive based on your guidance and advice is incredibly rewarding and educational. As the Joseph Joubert saying goes, "To teach is to learn twice."

I suspect that this is the philosophy behind the sundry wine blogs where the blogger wants to help you learn about the world of wine in some new or innovative way. There is a genuine desire to help spread the word and show others the same joy that the blogger feels when they enjoy wine. It's a sharing of enthusiasm and potentially inspirational to the next generation of wine lovers and sipsters.

This wine leads by example. It is the mentor to all Rieslings in BC. The same energy and enthusiasm that goes into making it inspires others to seek out and taste more Rieslings, or more wines from Tantalus, or more wines from the Kelowna south slopes region.

Or . . . all of the above.

WHITE

Wet streets. Damp jacket. Beautiful sunset peeking through the clouds.

UNSWORTH
VINEYARDS
2020
~ ISLAND MELODY ~
VANCOUVER ISLAND, BC VQA
12.3 % alc./vol. 750ml

UNSWORTH VINEYARDS ISLAND MELODY

WINERY PRICE: 🍷 🍷 🍷
BODY: LIGHT
SWEETNESS: DRY(ISH)
ATTITUDE: CLARITY

Pair with: Chicken Caesar salads, pear and Brie panini, singing in the rain

There are times when I can see clearly that the rain has gone. I can also see all of the obstacles in my way. Gone are those pesky dark clouds that had me blind. It's going to be a bright, bright wine today.

If you have that song* stuck in your head now, I will consider my work here done. That's exactly the feeling that I got sipping on this lovely wine from Vancouver Island. Tasting it was a beautiful sight.

BC's coast is the first place I ever lived where I met people who *liked* rain. A few of them loved it and missed it when it was not there. The sound of it was comforting to them. The swishing windshield wipers meant that they were close to home. Watching people struggle with umbrellas (clearly people who weren't from there) was amusing to them because they would never think to take shelter from something that they loved so much. But no matter how much they loved it, there was a noticeable lifting of the mood when it stopped raining and the sun came out.

Wet streets. Damp jacket. Beautiful sunset peeking through the clouds over English Bay. This wine is all of the beauty that is a rainy day.

*"I Can See Clearly Now" by Johnny Nash.

It could not have
been produced by
anyone else from
anywhere else.

vinAmité

Chanson d'amour

Family Estate Vineyard & Winery, Oliver, BC

A

VINAMITÉ CELLARS CHANSON D'AMOUR

WINERY PRICE: 🍷 🍷 🍷
BODY: LIGHT
SWEETNESS: DRY
ATTITUDE: LOVING

Pair with: Oysters, soft cheese, staring into your partner's eyes

I've always found that food tastes different to me when it's cooked at home compared to when I eat at restaurants. I don't recall eating in restaurants that often as a kid so when I did, it was a memorable experience. I remember that restaurant food tasted kind of predictable. It was good, but it just didn't have that special something. Maybe it was more salt than I was used to or perhaps it was more, or unfamiliar, spices. Something was different.

When I became a parent, feeding the kids was an important aspect of keeping them healthy. As a single parent, I learned to get a certain amount of joy from creating special meals that they enjoyed repeatedly. There was something satisfying about making food for people. Suddenly, I understood what my mother and grandmothers had done when they spent so much time making food for the family. They were sharing their love in the form of food, and that's why their home-cooked food tasted so good.

Everything about this wine that is nearly indescribable—the aromas, the textures, the flavours—makes it feel like a home-cooked meal. It could not have been produced by anyone else from anywhere else. Like Mom's cooking, it is unique and meant to be fulfilling as more than nutrition.

And when your kids grow to be teenagers who don't seem to care about anything you do, this wine will make for fantastic sipping while they do the dishes.

ROSÉ WINES

Oh rosé, you silly, unpredictable wine style. What is it that has made you so appealing, versatile, and crazy-popular over the past decade?

Rosé isn't just that nebulous grey area between the two poles of white and red that desperately hopes to appeal to both sides equally by giving a little of what each likes. Rosé is a completely different category of wine that has its own unique purpose in the sipster's cellar. There can be serious, dry versions and fun, easy-drinking versions. (I didn't say "slightly sweet," but you knew where I was going.) There are also versions that have the potential to get more interesting after they have been aged for a few years. True, not many wineries are dabbling in this yet, but hopefully there will be some more experiments in this direction.

What makes rosé really fascinating in BC is that it is still largely unexplored territory. It is the Wild West of the Wild West, open to new discoveries, potentials, and possibilities. For the adventurous sipster, every new rosé is an exciting possibility.

It's the same reason nobody bothers to do fast-food restaurant reviews.

Aasha Wines

Little Monster
2017 Syrah Rosé
SOUTH OKANAGAN

AASHA WINES LITTLE MONSTER ROSÉ

WINERY PRICE: ♟ ♟ ♟
BODY: MEDIUM
SWEETNESS: DRY
ATTITUDE: SLOW

Pair with: BBQ *chicken, light cheeses, long afternoons*

Low and slow is the mantra of the barbeque pit master. Low temperatures for a long time with smoke adding flavour and helping to preserve the meat at the same time. It's a natural cooking method that originated in Africa and lives on in the tradition of the American South.

The word *slow* can be interpreted as a bit derogatory when applied to a person, but when it is attached to food, that's something entirely different. Slow food is the opposite of fast food. Cooking something slowly builds more flavours than cooking something quickly. One could cook chicken by smoking it slowly in a smoker or microwave it in a fraction of the time. Which one is going to taste better? There is a reason why there are no microwaved food competitions on TV and it's the same reason nobody bothers to do fast-food restaurant reviews or share photos of fast food on social media. There is nothing special about fast food. Slow is special.

Describing this wine's attitude as slow is a compliment. This is not a rosé that is rushed out and delivered to the wine shop right off the bottling line. This one has taken its time.

ROSÉ

It was impossible
to listen to for
any length of time
without also starting
to laugh.

NORTHERN LIGHTS ESTATE WINERY NECHAKO CRUSH

WINERY PRICE: 🍷 🍷
BODY: MEDIUM
SWEETNESS: OFF-DRY
ATTITUDE: FUN FUN FUN!

Pair with: Turkey dinners, anything with goat cheese, amusement parks

This wine will bring a smile to your face. Seriously, this wine is one of those rollercoaster snapshots in a bottle, complete with your face frozen in mid-scream with your tongue hanging out. If you can't have a good time at an amusement park or fair, like the PNE, then you may have an allergy to fun. Take one of these Nechako Crush Rhubarb wines and call me in the morning.

Laughter and fun are contagious that way. The campus radio station at the university I attended had a set of records that contained nothing but the sound of people laughing. It was impossible to listen to for any length of time without also starting to laugh. This bottle of giggles will do the same thing. It will be the laugh track for your life as soon as you crack it open.

The more you sip, the more it will lighten the mood. Laughter is infectious. Since we have all learned a lot about being infectious over the past couple of years (yes, I went there), this is one wine that will be perfect for getting together and enjoying each other's company again.

Open a bottle and take in the aromas. The fun is about to begin.

ROSÉ

Or pause for
a moment if the
weather is good
at the top.

PEAK CELLARS PINOT NOIR ROSÉ

WINERY PRICE: 🍷 🍷 🍷
BODY: LIGHT
SWEETNESS: DRY
ATTITUDE: OUTDOORSY

Pair with: Rotisserie chicken, charcuterie, mountain air

This wine pairs beautifully with fresh mountain air. Every place has different air. Factors like elevation, proximity to water, vegetation, climate, and human industries all play a part in a place's environment and air quality. The BC coast has a temperate climate, dense rainforests, large mountains, and the constant presence of the Pacific Ocean. That makes the air on the coast a little more dense, a little saltier, and certainly a lot more humid. Hike to the top of the Stawamus Chief or Grouse Mountain and the air will change, thinning out slightly but noticeably with the higher altitude.

Though it is higher in elevation than the coast, the air in the Okanagan Valley near the lake might not be high enough up to capture that same freshness. You might have to drive or hike up a little higher to the top of Mount Kobau or Giant's Head. Or pause for a moment if the weather is good at the top of Apex, Baldy, or Big White in the winter. That is mountain air. The beautiful views that accompany such a climb also make for a beautiful accompaniment that will only heighten the experience (so to speak).

Have a sip and enjoy the view.

ROSÉ

RED WINES

Okay, here we go with the "serious" wines. Reds are supposedly the manly wines, the ones that attract the high-rolling collectors. Red wines command the most respect and attention at auctions and get written about endlessly in wine magazines with a verve that borders on pornographic. The reds from Bordeaux and Burgundy get the most attention in wine annuals because they are the highest echelons of possible achievement in the world of wine, even though both regions produce white wines too. "Look at how much more your investment would be worth now," they say. "The value of fine wines has outpaced the stock market by 400% since the 1990s!"

If you have skipped ahead to this section, ignoring the sparkings, whites, and rosés, because they aren't serious wines, all I can say is that you have missed out. There are just as many serious reds as there are capricious or silly reds. Just like in the other sections, there are reds for all different kinds of situations, moods, and environments.

However, you determine the true value of a wine. I hope you enjoy the search.

It's like they want to make sure nobody else crowds their hang the next time they visit.

ANCIENT HILL BACO NOIR

WINERY PRICE: 🍷 🍷 🍷
BODY: MEDIUM
SWEETNESS: DRY
ATTITUDE: WILD

Pair with: Heartfelt piano ballads, smoked sausages or fish, camping

---

BC has a lot of wilderness compared to other places. It only takes a couple hours of driving from Vancouver to reach a remote valley with no cell service and the echoing silence that can only come from a heavily forested mountain lake. Long-time residents of BC love these kinds of places. But if you ask them where exactly a particular spot is, they suddenly get vague. "Oh, you know, it's just off of Route 3 just before Manning Park." Or "You've been to Lynn Valley's demonstration forest? Yeah, somewhere in there . . ." It's like they want to make sure nobody else crowds their hang the next time they visit.

This wine is as unique as those quiet wilderness spots. Not everyone likes to be so far out in the wild and that's okay. Not everyone will enjoy this wine to the same degree either, but that's okay too. Adventurous sipsters will enjoy and cling to the wilder aspects of this wine that make it endlessly interesting. Just like most of the world's wilderness areas, Baco is becoming a lot less common than it used to be in BC.

If you need to know, Ancient Hill is off on its own on the site of a historic vineyard on Black Mountain in Kelowna. You know, somewhere near the airport.

RED

Though the world
might appear to be
going the way of the
burning dumpster.

ANTHONY BUCHANAN FUBAR

WINERY PRICE: 🍷 🍷 🍷 🍷
BODY: MEDIUM
SWEETNESS: DRY
ATTITUDE: F*CK IT

Pair with: Herb-crusted pork tenderloin, BBQ *chicken thighs, contemplating the bizarre nature of humanity*

When the shit hits the fan, I'm pretty sure that the products you'll need to cope will be advertised on YouTube. But honestly, when you get that feeling of resignation where there is nothing left to do but just surrender yourself to the fates, this is the wine you want to be drinking.

There are a lot of reasons for that. First, the name. If you don't know what it stands for, I will not spoil it for you. Either search it online or (a far better use of your time) watch the classic movie *Saving Private Ryan*. Suffice it to say that it is potentially relevant to the circumstances involved in your aforementioned surrender to the fates. It might not be that relevant, but once that sense of surrender really sets in, well, it doesn't really matter anymore now, does it?

Secondly, this wine has everything that you'd want for just such an occasion. It has tons of complex aromas and flavours, a beautiful colour, and it isn't harsh on the palate when you sip. It's got some serious texture to it as well, so it won't just disappear on you when you pair food with it.

That's not to say that you should abandon all hope. Far from it. If that's where you're at, there are other beverages to slam back with that in mind. No, if anything, this wine will remind you that there are still good people out there. Though the world might appear to be going the way of the burning dumpster, this wine will show you glorious possibilities you never knew existed. It is a reimagining in a wine glass.

Everything is going to be fine. I'll just be here sipping my wine.

RED

In the same fastidious and zealous way that someone might continue to play an old video game.

ARROWLEAF

2019
ZWEIGELT
bc vqa okanagan valley

ARROWLEAF ZWEIGELT

WINERY PRICE: 🍷 🍷 🍷
BODY: MEDIUM
SWEETNESS: DRY
ATTITUDE: FAITHFUL

Pair with: Pizza with spicy toppings, pork or chicken skewers, classic video games

---

Zweigelt is like Pinot Noir with an attitude problem. Though it might not be as familiar a grape as Merlot or Syrah, it is the happy medium (literally) between the two. It carries the dark fruit of Merlot with the peppery edge of Syrah in a totally approachable way. The Okanagan Valley has some fantastic examples of it, and thank goodness for the stalwart wineries who continue to produce it.

Wineries that bottle a single-variety Zweigelt *really* like Zweigelt in the same fastidious and zealous way that someone continues to play an old video game, clings to their dying (and unsupported) Blackberry smartphone, or continues to drive an old car that they have owned for decades, not wanting to give up just yet. That isn't nostalgia, that's dedication. It is rare and not for everyone, but sipsters can appreciate that level of dedication, even if they themselves aren't quite as into it. The question then is not, "Why would someone love this grape so much?" but "What is it about this grape that can draw this kind of devotion?" If you haven't tried Arrowleaf's Zweigelt, you are missing out on appreciating the fervour they have put into years of making wine from this rare grape.

This is what devotion tastes like.

RED

If everyone got
along, there would
be no tension.

DEAD END GAME OVER

WINERY PRICE: 🍷 🍷 🍷 🍷 🍷
BODY: FULL
SWEETNESS: DRY
ATTITUDE: DRAMATIC

Pair with: Prime rib, hearty stews, horror movies

This is a dramatic wine, in a way that isn't immediately obvious. The word *drama* often has bad connotations, as if it were something to be avoided between people. Certainly, there are times when too much drama can be taxing. But without drama, life would become boring.

Drama is what adds constructive conflict and dimension to life. If everyone got along, there would be no tension. We would all go happily through our day thinking everything was awesome.

Anyone who has been around teenagers knows that it doesn't take much to create drama. It does take a brilliant person to create *good* or even *exceptionally good* drama. Perhaps this is something that we are losing in our society today with so much social media, a solidly un-dramatic medium, at the centre of our lives. One does not simply type words onto a Boomerang image to create drama. One does that for comedic memes, not dramatic tension. Perhaps the ultimate drama happens in plays. Yes, Shakespeare, but also hundreds of more modern works like *Never Swim Alone* by Canadian playwright Daniel MacIvor.

What makes this wine dramatic is the tension between its elements. It has beautiful aromas but also enough tannins to turn your teeth into leather after one sip. It has beautiful colour in the glass, which hopefully the glass likes just as much as you do because it will be stained that colour. Oh, *drama*.

Like all good dramas, this one ends with a wonderfully long and thought-provoking finish. Not an easy thing to do with wine.

RED

You've just gotten home, the kids are hungry (or worse, you are hangry).

DEEP ROOTS WINERY GAMAY

WINERY PRICE: 🍷 🍷 🍷
BODY: MEDIUM
SWEETNESS: DRY
ATTITUDE: HOME SWEET HOME

Pair with: Chicken panini, grilled pork chops with a fruity BBQ *sauce, almost anything home cooked*

What to do? What to do? What to do . . . for dinner?

When it seems like the options are endless but the choices are limited, making a meal at home can be anxiety-inducing. You've just gotten home, the kids are hungry (or worse, you are *hangry*). At last, you manage to find a combination in your cupboards that kind of makes sense. Time for the pantry-raid of wines.

It is entirely likely that whatever you come up with, this Gamay will happily accompany it. Unless you have filet mignon in your fridge, ready to go at a moment's notice, you will probably come up with something that is satisfying if not only in taste, then also in the pride it conjures. Pride that you made this meal with nothing more than a series of ingredients you found in the back of your pantry that you'd forgotten about, a couple of pots, and a quick Google search to find the right combination of herbs. You are not a trained chef but gosh darn it, you could be. This is the chef's black box competition for real and you just took top prize.

This Gamay works because it has everything you could possibly need to pair with that home-cooked meal. You could argue that the acidity, flavours, and hint of spice in this wine make it a meal unto itself, and I would agree with you on that. Put another way, if versatility is in fashion, then this wine is walking the runway.

RED

EX NIHILO

Questions like, "I wonder what it was like back then?" or "Why don't we do things like this now?"

EX NIHILO MERLOT

WINERY PRICE: ♟ ♟ ♟ ♟ ♟
BODY: FULL
SWEETNESS: DRY
ATTITUDE: ELEGANT RUSTIC

Pair with: Grilled veggies, marinated steaks, a cigar on a porch rocking chair

Merlot has become BC's antique grape variety to some degree. Since the 1990s, when it proved that it could grow well here, nearly every winery has made wine from it. Not all Merlots are created equal and, if you've read Volume 1 of *Sipster's*, you'll know that not a lot of them were included in that one. Many are frankly not interesting enough to merit any special attention. It is almost the vanilla of the BC wine world.

So when an interesting one is included here, you can be sure that it deserves it.

The phrase "they don't make things like they used to" means a lot to some people, particularly those who appreciate and cherish antique furniture. There is something solid about the construction, the history that the furniture has been through with previous owners, and the little fixes that may have taken place to keep it in good shape. The best antiques stand out because they are the most well made, most appreciated, and best taken care of.

It is clear that Ex Nihilo has taken care of their Merlot in this way, "like they used to." There are aromas that will take you back to a time long ago, before you were consciously aware of things, maybe even before you were born. You'll find textures in this wine that you will want to run your fingers over. Tasting it will bring on questions like, "I wonder what it was like back then?" or "Why don't we do things like this now?"

Not every wine can function like a time machine. When you find a wine that can, it is a beautiful experience.

RED

It needs a lot of
land and people
with enough
vision to find new
places to ranch.

FORT BERENS ESTATE WINERY RESERVE CABERNET FRANC

WINERY PRICE: 🍷 🍷 🍷 🍷
BODY: MEDIUM
SWEETNESS: DRY
ATTITUDE: RANCHER

Pair with: Striploin steak, homemade burgers, riding the range

---

As any rancher can tell you, they are not farmers. They are ranchers. There is a difference. Farmers grow food from the ground or otherwise procure it from animals through milking or gathering eggs. Ranchers maintain herds of animals—cows mostly—for the production of meat. Ranching has a long history in the Okanagan Valley, which was used to transport beef herds to the miners in the Cariboo region and then as a site of large ranches in the late nineteenth century. There is nothing showy about ranching. It needs a lot of land and people with enough vision to find new places to do it. Not everyone is cut out for it.

There is an element of showiness that affects wines made in big wine regions. The wines of Bordeaux attract huge prices and therefore a lot of attention. Napa Valley had to stand out and they did so with big wines made with Cabernet Sauvignon and Chardonnay. Within BC, the Okanagan Valley had to stand out amongst the international competition and developed a very ostentatious style.

Being outside of the Okanagan Valley, Fort Berens is really BC wine's most remote "ranch." The Cabernet Franc, which is grown mostly on the winery's property in Lillooet, BC, is perfectly not-showy in that humble rancher style. It has all of the goodness of Cabernet Franc—the slightly spicy aromas, the beautiful savoury flavours, the smooth texture—but manages to be thoroughly un-showy. It is the real deal.

RED

The solid, trusted
uncle who will
happily loan you
money (or his car)
if you need it.

HERE'S THE THING
VINEYARDS
Clearly
CABERNET FRANC
British Columbia

HERE'S THE THING VINEYARDS CLEARLY CABERNET FRANC

WINERY PRICE: 🍷 🍷 🍷
BODY: MEDIUM
SWEETNESS: DRY
ATTITUDE: AMICABLE

Pair with: Kabobs and grilled veggies, sautéed eggplant, reading under a blanket

Cabernet Franc is like the weird uncle in a wealthy family: a little unpredictable, always entertaining, and, when it really counts, able to deliver on promises. Even though it might be a weird way to deliver them.

Cousin Cabernet Sauvignon—Cab Franc's son with mild-mannered Aunty Sauvignon Blanc—is the awesome older cousin, the one that has all the cool stuff before you do, and who seems popular and able to handle anything at the family reunion. When it's time to jump in the pool, Cabernet Sauvignon does the best dives. Nobody notices the weird Uncle Franc in the shallow end, chilling out and relaxing all cool. My point here is that Cab Franc in BC is not always looked upon with the gusto it deserves. It is respected but not admired. This Cab Franc is not the huge tannic monster that Cab Sauv can become if not carefully supervised at the fermentation party.

Here's the Thing's Cabernet Franc is the solid, trusted uncle who will happily loan you money (or his car) if you need it. Food pairings? No problem. The amicability of this wine is off the charts in a beautifully refined way that only a close family member with a huge reserve of trust in you can give. Families can be together for many years and yet they forget that some-times, not everything goes as planned. Happily, this Cabernet Franc will be there in the wings when you need it the most.

Plus, family reunions will be that much more special.

Oh, it's just
down the road!

HORSESHOE FOUND PINOT NOIR

WINERY PRICE: 🍷 🍷 🍷 🍷
BODY: MEDIUM
SWEETNESS: DRY
ATTITUDE: REJUVENATING

Pair with: Fire-grilled porterhouse with mushroom sauce, rotisserie chicken, romantic alfresco dinners

Me: What do you recommend?
Server: If you like local wines, you might try the Horseshoe Found Pinot Noir.
Me: I'm sorry, who?
Server: Oh, I'm sorry, are you new to BC wine?
Me: Well, no, uh, I, um, have written some books on . . . er, so where is this winery again?
Server: Oh, it's just down the road!

Sipsters like learning about wine, but if there is one thing we absolutely *love*, it's discovering fantastic new wines. It was late summer 2021 dining at Row Fourteen in Cawston when the server suggested this wine to me and my dinner companion. She, equally knowledgeable about BC wines, was just as surprised as I was. It was a legit sipster moment of discovery.

Before the bottle was brought to the table, a quick internet search revealed *absolutely nothing* about this winery or the wine. It was almost a blind-tasting experience. Knowing only that it was "down the road" (so, somewhere in the Similkameen Valley near Cawston) and that it was Pinot Noir, we were able to freely taste a beautiful wine unencumbered by any other information. Strangely, it was beautifully freeing. This wine was the star of our dining experience.

It also reminded me that even in the most familiar places, stores, or restaurants, wine adventures can always be just a question away. Next time you are at a great restaurant, ask your server for their suggestion.

One of those rare
examples of buying
a Ferrari for the
price of a Honda.

HUGGING
TREE
WINERY

20
19   MOONCHILD MERLOT

BC VQA SIMILKAMEEN VALLEY

RED WINE, PRODUCT OF CANADA   13.6% alc./vol. 750 ml
VIN ROUGE, PRODUIT DU CANADA

HUGGING TREE WINERY MOONCHILD MERLOT

WINERY PRICE: 🍷 🍷 🍷
BODY: MEDIUM
SWEETNESS: DRY
ATTITUDE: EAGER

Pair with: Lamb skewers, filet mignon, unicorn spotting

This is one of those "Start the car!" wines where the price is so far below the quality of the wine that buying it feels like stealing. This is one of those rare examples of buying a Ferrari for the price of a Honda.

What gives a wine its value? That depends on who you ask. For most wine lovers, beautiful flavours and complex aromas are important. The difference between a $10 Merlot and a $40 Merlot isn't just $30 extra. In theory, an inexpensive $10 Merlot will not have a lot of complex flavours and will taste exactly the same from sip to sip, bottle to bottle, and vintage to vintage. If predictability is your jam, let that be your wine and be proud of the fact that you don't have to spend a lot.

If a little unpredictability and adventurous taste is more your style, then it may take a little more money per bottle to find something that has more complex flavours, a finer texture, longer finish, and better potential for aging (if that's something that you like to do). BC's wines tend to be on the higher end of the prices on the store shelves so people looking for inexpensive wines sometimes avoid looking at local wines. The real unicorns of the wine world are those that have beautifully deep and complex flavours but with a price that seems too good to be true.

This wine is a unicorn. Consider yourself lucky if you even spot this Merlot on the shelf.

RED

When it seems
that the world is
just too caged in,
too simplified,
and too orderly.

KALALA ZWEIGELT

WINERY PRICE: 🍷 🍷 🍷
BODY: MEDIUM
SWEETNESS: DRY
ATTITUDE: GRAPES GONE WILD

Pair with: Pulled pork, Cajun-spiced chicken, weekend getaways

---

Discipline is a good thing. It's good to be able to focus on a task and get it done, on time if possible, but at the very least, done and done well. Then there are also times when being focused, on-task, or overly disciplined gets old and burn-out or fatigue sets in. It's time to let loose.

Going wild is a natural part of our lives. There are times when it seems that the world is just too caged in, too simpli-fied, and too orderly. When it gets like this, something needs to be done to break it up, disrupt the flow, and stop the monotony. The novelty that disruptions can give us is thrilling, enliven-ing, and even rejuvenating. Wild times are what we need to push the reset button on our brains.

The Zweigelt grape has given Kalala a great starting point to do this. Their portfolio has all the stalwart grape varieties like Merlot and Gewurztraminer, but it's the Zweigelt, a grape that isn't that well known, that has consistently pushed the wild button. There are so many crazy, spicy aromas and scrump-tiously savoury flavours wrapped up in it that you'll swear you were being filmed doing something silly on YouTube.

RED

Each time you talk
or visit, you pick
right up where you
left off as if no time
has gone by at all.

LARIANA
CELLARS

EIGHTEEN
OKANAGAN VALLEY
BC VQA

14.2% alc./vol.   750 ml

LARIANA CELLARS *NUMBERED SERIES*

WINERY PRICE: 🍷 🍷 🍷 🍷
BODY: MEDIUM +
SWEETNESS: DRY
ATTITUDE: FAMILIAR

Pair with: Stargazing with friends, bistecca alla Fiorentina, very special occasions

Some friendships depend on the amount of time you spend with that person. Better friends are around more and so you become closer.

There are also friendships that transcend time. It doesn't matter if it's been two weeks since you've spoken to them or twenty years. Each time you talk or visit, you pick right up where you left off as if no time has gone by at all. These friendships are dependable and last a lifetime. They are the least likely to be severed because of things like distance, busy lives, or pandemic isolation.

Lariana Cellars' vintage blends are among the few wines in BC that can pick up right where you left off the last time that you tasted them. This tiny vineyard on the American border in Osoyoos produces a wine that feels like you've known it forever. It doesn't matter what vintage it is, it's going to be there to reconnect with you.

The list of descriptors that one could write about the nose of this wine could fill a book of its own. Another book would be required for the flavours and the finish. Not unlike the sheer complexity of a long-term friendship. Thousands of shared memories, inside jokes, things learned from each other, time spend together or apart, and tragedies experienced are all represented by the diversity of fruit aromas, the savoury fullness of the palate, the sting of the alcohol, and the long-distance finish.

This is true grand cru–level wine. Open it for those precious grand cru–level friends.

RED

You are going to
turn heads and
you're going to
feel great.

LE VIEUX PIN SYRAH "CUVÉE VIOLETTE"

WINERY PRICE: 🍷 🍷 🍷 🍷
BODY: FULL
SWEETNESS: DRY
ATTITUDE: NIGHT AT THE OPERA

Pair with: Marinated steak, grilled duck with hoisin, formalwear

---

Some wines are great for casual receptions. Some are fantastic for dinners at home, as pizza wines, sipping on the patio, or whatever other cliché the wine-shop staff spout to get you to make a purchase.

This wine is not one of those. It is entirely in a class of its own. None of the clichés apply.

If most wines are casual clothes, this wine is a ballgown or tuxedo. I don't mean a little black dress or a blazer-over-T-shirt. This is the all-out dress-up night with your best pair of pumps or wingtips. You are going to turn heads, and you're going to feel great. This is special occasion wine at its best.

It also goes beyond the clothing. It encompasses everything from the undergarments to the accessories. The wine's starbright purple hue as it swirls is the complex sparkle of your finest matching jewelry. The profound aromas are the expensive perfume or cologne that you splash on just before leaving. Add your matching clutch or pocket square and you are ready for the great night out that this wine inspires.

Don't forget your best playlist for the soundtrack.

RED

They were sure that
you'd fit in with
the kids there even
though those kids
didn't know squat
about living in the
real world.

MORAINE CLIFFHANGER RED

WINERY PRICE: 🍷 🍷 🍷
BODY: FULL
SWEETNESS: DRY
ATTITUDE: HOMEY

Pair with: Bluegrass, dancing around a fire, gourmet burgers

Going home is something that not everyone can do, at least literally, if home is the place where you were born and grew up. Some people leave their homes for other provinces or countries. Perhaps your parents sold the home where you spent most of your childhood because they had to move back to the city where there was stable income and it didn't matter that it was a new school, they were sure that you'd fit in with the kids there even though those kids didn't know squat about living in the real world because their sheltered urban existence precluded them from really understanding the truth about . . .

So, um, anyway, this wine is a great way to reconnect with that feeling of home, even if the location might change over time. The smell of familiarity, the instant sense of relaxation, and hitting pause on your anxieties—all those things that can accompany entering the place where nothing can do you harm and all is unconditionally forgiven. Home can be where family is, but it can just as easily be a school, a restaurant, or even a special part of town. It's wherever that sense of belonging is felt.

Wherever that place is, this wine brings that sense of home. It's a lovely feeling on which to sip.

RED

Sleepers are cars that look normal on the outside but have crazy overpowered engines.

PLATINUM BENCH ESTATE WINERY SYRAH BLOCK 23

WINERY PRICE: 🍷 🍷 🍷 🍷
BODY: MEDIUM
SWEETNESS: DRY
ATTITUDE: HIDDEN

Pair with: Pepper steak, grilled steak, steak sandwich, steak frites, dreaming of steak

Car lovers know what a sleeper is. Sleepers are cars that look normal on the outside but have crazy overpowered, possibly turbocharged, engines and other performance features not visible from the outside.

This wine is Platinum Bench's sleeper wine. Yes, it looks just like the other wines in their portfolio with the same double labels on the front. "Oh, don't they also do a nice Gamay?" Yes, they do. It's lovely. "And that *bread*! Have you tried it?" Yes, many times. It almost got its own chapter in this book.

Put this Syrah on the tasting bar, or even better, on your dinner table, and all other wines will get left in the dust. This wine really should not be such a surprise. Platinum Bench has been producing solid wines for many years now, and they are located in the middle of the Black Sage Bench, one of the best wine-growing regions in the country, not just BC. This wine is no rat rod (i.e. a powerful engine hidden underneath a body made with repurposed parts and rusted-out panels). It's the real deal Syrah with all of the flavour depth, elegance, spice, and fruit that we have learned to expect from that variety grown in BC.

When tested on my table, it went from zero to "holy crap that's good" in 1.3 sips.

RED

Suddenly, the pressure to get things done at a certain time isn't important.

Vancouver Island Wines

RATHJEN
CELLARS

PINOT NOIR 2019
Saison Vineyard

RATHJEN CELLARS PINOT NOIR

WINERY PRICE: 🍷 🍷 🍷 🍷
BODY: MEDIUM
SWEETNESS: DRY
ATTITUDE: CHILL

Pair with: Margherita pizza, mushroom tortellini, relaxing

Relaxing is not always easy. Some of us are clearly better at it than others. For many years, I didn't appreciate relaxing because it seemed that I rarely ever got a chance to do it. Working in the wine industry meant working on long weekends and time off when nobody else had time off. Getting together with anyone or spending time with my family had to be scheduled around other things.

Now that I have a little more time to relax, the experience of stretching out and maybe reading a book or listening to a podcast while doing nothing else feels fantastic. Suddenly, the pressure to get things done at a certain time isn't important. Things will be as they are. It's a wonderful, freeing feeling and it's a great reset for the brain to approach the upcoming work week in the same way. Things will get done. Stressing over them probably isn't helpful.

The total velvety smoothness of this wine will invite you to that same feeling of relaxation. There is nothing hurried about it at all—no pushy aromas or obtuse flavours to jar your palate into wanting to eat more or pair certain foods. This wine will happily go where you want and not push you where you don't want to go. It's a totally relaxing experience in a glass and a perfect accompaniment for comfort foods of all kinds.

RED

Classical music,
like wine for many
years, has had public
relations problems.

SOLVERO PINOT NOIR

WINERY PRICE: 🍷 🍷 🍷 🍷
BODY: MEDIUM
SWEETNESS: DRY
ATTITUDE: DISCIPLINED

Pair with: Soft cheese, pork chops with mushroom sauce, Beethoven piano sonatas

---

This wine is a beautifully constructed sonata.

Classical music, like wine for many years, has had public relations problems. Both have been criticized for being snobbish, elitist, or worse, that completely overused word: *pretentious*. It makes learning more about wine (or classical music) difficult and forces some people, I believe, to give up on it completely rather than feeling free to explore on their own. When people give up on something, they can often feel bitter about it and then for the rest of their lives, they will deride other people for knowing about it themselves.

Historically, wine and classical music are a little like the worst attitudes on social media. If you choose to voice an opinion, any opinion, on social media, be prepared to be belittled, berated, chided for being "clearly wrong" or told "u have no idea what *your* talking about."

This is unfortunate because there are so many beautiful wines and so much beautiful classical music. With the best of them, you don't even have to know anything about them in advance to understand that what you are experiencing is fantastic. It could be a revelatory experience, a "sine qua non" of the repertoire, or whatever other douchey old phrase you want to use. You will still know it is good. You will know and nobody will prove you wrong, nor will anyone's opinion of it matter to you.

No matter how much or how little you know about wine (or think you know), when you try this wine, you will understand. It is a new classic.

Although this might be news to some of you, they do make other wines as well.

SYNCHROMESH STORM HAVEN CABERNET FRANC

WINERY PRICE: 🍷 🍷 🍷 🍷 🍷
BODY: MEDIUM
SWEETNESS: DRY
ATTITUDE: ELUSIVE

Pair with: BBQ *pork ribs, roast beef, enjoying the fruits of your labours*

Me: "I found a Synchromesh Cab Franc!"
Friend: "Synchromesh? Wow! Have you tried their Rieslings?"
Me: "Yeah, I've tried them."
Friend: "Holy crap, they're fantastic!"
Me: "Well, yes, I agree, but this one is—"
Friend: "It was so austere, but the flavours were off the charts!"
Me: "Yeah, this one too. Except it's a Cabernet Franc."
Friend: "Oh . . . You mean you didn't get a Riesling?"
Me: "No. It's a red. You know, a Cabernet Franc."
Friend: "Huh. Cool. Okay."

Sometimes being known for one thing is a great thing. Other times, it overshadows the other great things that you do. Nobody will dispute that this winery is fast becoming the benchmark for South Okanagan Rieslings. Although this might be news to some of you, they do make other wines as well.

It's difficult to believe that a winery that could put so much care and attention into one style of wine would simply ignore the others in their portfolio. Cabernet Franc has been a part of the lineup at Synchromesh for many vintages and surely receives as much care and attention as their Rieslings and Pinot Noirs.

This Cabernet Franc truly is a testament to that.

RED

DESSERT WINES

I believe that sweet wines are needlessly saddled with a thick layer of guilt. Perhaps this comes from everything else that is sweet being wrapped in that same package. "Oh, I can't have that—there's too much sugar." "Chocolate is just too sweet for me." We seem to equate it with a guilty pleasure that we are not supposed to enjoy.

Yes, processed sugar is addictive. There are debates about how much it is addictive when compared to narcotics or alcohol, but the research points to it being very addictive. Sugar is something that we all crave at some point even though it may not be the best thing for us.

Perhaps it comes down to a misunderstanding as to where the sugar in sweet wines comes from. Dessert wines are sweet because they've retained the natural sugars from the grapes. In BC, a common way to make sweet wines is to let the grapes freeze on the vine to make Icewine. Sometimes grapes will be left on the vine to concentrate without freezing, and that can be made into a late harvest wine. Sometimes the wines are fortified with extra alcohol part-way through fermentation when there is still a lot of sugar left over. Port-style wines are made in this fashion. In each of these methods, the sweetness comes from the grapes and not from adding processed sugar.

Hopefully, that makes enjoying these wines a little more guilt-free.

Antiques can be
quite profound.

D'ANGELO ESTATE WINERY DOLCE VITA ROSSO

WINERY PRICE: 🍷 🍷 FOR 200 ML
                   🍷 🍷 🍷 🍷 FOR 750 ML
BODY: FULL
SWEETNESS: MEDIUM
ATTITUDE: ANTIQUE

Pair with: Blue cheese, roasted hazelnuts, online buying sprees

---

When I was growing up, my parents frequented antique stores, where they bought many everyday items. Everything in those stores just seemed old to me, but this fit with the house where we lived at the time, which was built before Confederation.

People collect antiques for various reasons that range from the "They don't build them like they used to" past-equals-quality formula to "This could be worth something someday" investment opportunity. In between is an appreciation for craftmanship done with less technology and the look and feel of an item that is connected to a time before our own lives. Antiques can be quite profound.

This wine has that look and feel (in the form of the aromas and flavours) of a classic, high-quality antique. Tasting it feels like a step back in time to when winemaking was simpler, perhaps. Or at least less intruded upon by technology. This wine is not rustic in any way and is supremely refined and so well-proportioned and balanced that it will really make you wonder, how did they do it?

I later learned that my parents were trying to save money rather than fulfill any desire to get in touch with the past or purchase a potential investment. But from all those old things we lived with, I learned to appreciate the past. When a wine gives me that same perspective, it is quite a moving experience. This is one of those special wines.

DESSERT

I like to think of the
desire in its name
as being lustfully
directed at cheese.

FORBIDDEN FRUIT WINERY
POMME DESIREE

WINERY PRICE: 🍷 🍷 🍷 FOR 375 ML
BODY: FULL
SWEETNESS: SWEET
ATTITUDE: KISSY

Pair with: Cheese, yellow Indian curries, making out with your sweetie

---

In the context of Canadian dining rituals, sweet wines can be a bit of a mystery. Canadians produce some of the most outstanding dessert wines in the world but purchase very little of it and consume even less of whatever they do purchase. (Be honest, how many dessert wines do you have in your collection that you haven't used yet because you haven't found the right occasion?) Sweet wines have their place and when you find one that suits you, the indulgence is its own reward.

This is not a wine so much as it is a love letter written in fruit.

Technically, it isn't a wine at all, if we go with the definition of wine as being only made from grapes. It is made with organic apples in a sweet dessert-style wine. I like to think of the *desire* in its name as being lustfully directed at cheese. This wine loves cheese. All kinds of cheese, as well as some lightly sweet, fruity desserts.

Then there's the way the huge amount of acidity in this wine will make you pucker up, as if getting ready for that special kiss. This wine is love in a bottle, the precursor to romance, and the foreplay to all of your after-dinner activities.

Every flavour is within easy reach, and you won't have to stray far from your cozy blanket to get it.

Marionette

Lumière D'Hiver
2017

vin doux naturel

MARIONETTE LUMIÈRE D'HIVER RED

WINERY PRICE: 🍷 🍷 🍷 🍷 FOR 375 ML
BODY: FULL
SWEETNESS: SWEET
ATTITUDE: SELF-CARE

Pair with: Berry cobbler, fruity gelato, a fluffy blanket in front of a fireplace

This wine has everything you need for a relaxing sip by the fireplace during a snowstorm and nothing that you don't need. It has the comfortable chair, fluffy warm blanket, and table to hold your wineglass within easy reach. This wine has that balance of needs too—all the good things a sweet wine should have without any of the bad things.

It is made in the style of a French vin doux naturel, which means that it had alcohol added to it shortly after fermentation got started, leaving a lot of the grapes' original sweetness, fruity flavours, and no harsh tannins. The result is a beautiful wine with fruit flavours wrapped up gently in a gorgeously smooth package that you can sip all evening while reading near the fire during a cold winter night. It has enough flavour to be widely appealing without any of those hard-to-handle elements intruding on anyone's tastes. Every flavour is within easy reach, and you won't have to stray far from your cozy blanket to get it.

If Port has Stilton, Cognac has cigars, and Icewine has chocolate as their classic pairings, then this wine should be the classic pairing for a cozy evening by the fireplace.

DESSERT

SIPSTERS' CODE OF CONDUCT

As sipsters, we acknowledge that we are all individuals with unique taste preferences. Nobody is more of an expert on the way you enjoy wine than you are. Hence I have drafted a new Sipsters' Code of Conduct for enjoying wine.

Share your wines, even the special bottles. If someone is interested in a wine, they will likely appreciate it as well. Enjoying something fantastic together is what being a sipster is all about.

You do not know everything about wine and you never will. Remember in college when your friends asked you wine questions because you were the "wine expert" in the group? Looking back, how much do you think you knew then, and have you learned more since? Yeah, thought so.

Share your knowledge when it is appropriate. Nobody likes a know-it-all, but people do appreciate help when they need it. Knowing the difference is key to being a sipster.

Do not disparage wines that you do not like. All wine, no matter the quality level, could be someone's favourite bottle.

Enjoy the wine you're with. Never let the opportunity go by to enjoy the pleasures of experiencing wine.

GRAPE VARIETIES OF BRITISH COLUMBIA

Want to start an argument at a wine tasting? Ask anyone, "What are the best grapes for making wine in BC?"

Some parts of the world (mostly in Europe) have figured out what grapes work the best in their regions. Some of them figured it out a long time ago (such as Burgundy in the thirteenth century) and some of them are newer and evolved a little more recently (such as Bordeaux in the nineteenth century). Other regions haven't really settled on one and grow a select set of wine grapes (Germany, Austria, and Alsace) while others grow a lot of them and are not really that concerned with which varieties they actually are. (Portugal: "It's sweet and fortified. Shut up.")

That's the Old World (as we say in the wine industry) where they have a long history of growing grapes and making wine. The New World regions (i.e. places that are not Europe) started growing grapes and making wine much more recently. Some of them have not yet decided which grape varieties work best (or, from a more practical point of view, *sell* best). But some of them have: New Zealand deliberately staked a claim on Sauvignon Blanc. Napa Valley is big Cabernet Sauvignon country while Oregon is betting on Pinot Noir. South Africa has Pinotage locked up really well, and Australia can claim Shiraz with a good amount of authority. But what about other newer regions like Washington State, Ontario, or China? What about BC?

Hold that thought.

Some of the Old World regions determined their best grape varieties prior to the Enlightenment and much of it was trial and error over centuries. People used their intuition, their senses, and their knowledge of the land gleaned from generations of accumulated knowledge to figure out their grapes. This is where our *experience* in tasting the wines counts for something and where science might not be all that helpful. Our appreciation for the *art* of winemaking (through our sense of taste) determines what grows best in a given location and then science figures out why it works later on. As Jonah Lehrer suggested in his fantastic book *Proust Was a Neuroscientist*, science often learns what artists have already figured out through their experiences. Critically, he also points out that both science and art are equally important when trying to describe what we actually experience. "Physics is useful for describing quarks and galaxies, neuroscience is useful for describing the brain, and art is useful for describing our actual experience." *

Vineyard owners, and any wineries that grow their own grapes, will answer the "What grapes are the best grapes?" question by listing all of the grapes *they* grow. To stand behind their products, they really have to believe they are growing the best grapes, otherwise they would never have planted them. Or, if they purchased a vineyard that was already planted, they would still give the same answer to justify why they have not replanted with something better. Wineries do the same thing. No winery will ever say, "Well, you know, the Cabernet Sauvignon that we grow in the northern Okanagan really isn't that good so you probably shouldn't buy it." Those are wineries that will go out of business very soon. How did they choose those grapes in the first place? Probably a combination of factors from careful scientific study, consultation with neighbours, market conditions, and their own personal wine preferences. Most likely, one of those factors will have dominated over the others in selecting the grapes that a vineyard has started with. That does not mean that those are actually the best grapes for the region.

Our experiences, as people who ultimately taste and judge the resulting wines, should count for something. As tasters with our own unique experiences, we have a say in what wineries in BC produce. Sipsters and all wine lovers around the world

*p. 191–92

actually have a say in what wines are grown in which regions simply by choosing to purchase wines that are worthy. Cabernet Sauvignon in Ontario? No, thank you. Please stop growing it. Cabernet Franc? Yes, please! I'll take a case. Syrah in the south Okanagan? Take my money now!

If it will sell, wineries will continue production or even plant more. If it languishes on the shelf year after year, somebody will notice and eventually stop production or find a way to blend it away into something more interesting. That winnowing process can take a while unless someone has a runaway success with one particular grape variety. So far, that has not yet happened in BC because the industry is still a little too young and most wineries easily sell anything they make. The debate continues.

The short list of grape varieties that follows may also contain the relevant regions where those varieties stand out with unique characteristics. This is based on two things: tasting experiences and observations about the industry.

I have been lucky to have had many experiences with these grape varieties over the years and have enjoyed comparing wines made from them across different regions. For example, Merlot from the Okanagan is pretty consistently good. But Merlot from Naramata shows something just a little more special—more spice and complexity and therefore a more interesting tasting experience. Why is this? Lots of theoretical reasons but nothing really explainable by science. Could be the geology. Could be the western-facing vineyards. Could be the elevation. Could be the presence of the lake in combination with any or all of the previous attributes. Will we ever know for sure? Probably not. Is that the point? Not really. The point is that wines from these places show something just a little different than those from other places.

The second part is observing the portfolios of wineries over the years and seeing patterns. Almost every winery on Kelowna's south benches now produces a Riesling. Isn't that interesting? Some, like Tantalus and Kitsch, have even made it the focal point of their portfolios. Maybe Riesling does something special in that region and people have made a point of buying it more often? Interesting. There are a lot of velvety Pinot Noirs being made in the Cowichan Valley. Maybe that's a good place to grow that variety?

The list of places I have chosen to include is not exhaustive nor does it suggest that there can't be other fantastic examples of that variety grown in other regions. They are simply observations from experience. You may have had different experiences, and that's great because those are just as worthy of being passed along to the wineries. Tell them how much you love a wine through social media or at a winemaker's dinner. Your experiences count too.

WHITE GRAPE VARIETIES

BC has been making world-class white wines for a lot longer than it has red wines. Even still, compared to other wine regions of the world, we're still talking about only a short amount of time—maybe twenty years, give or take a half-decade. Here are the standout white grape varieties for making wines along with some suggestions for building flights for tastings.

RIESLING (KELOWNA, LAKE COUNTRY, SIMILKAMEEN VALLEY)

This grape could be the most potent purveyor of BC's reputation internationally. Even though other regions have already staked a claim on a style of Riesling (Germany, Alsace, parts of Australia), the amazing thing about Riesling is that it is strikingly different wherever it is grown. It reflects that elusive terroir extremely well, possibly better than any other white wine grape.

In BC, the regions around Kelowna and Lake Country have demonstrated some fantastic Rieslings. Tantalus Vineyards, their vineyard site, and their clone of Riesling has been mentioned in *The World Atlas of Wine*, one of the most internationally respected books on wine's geography (and therefore terroir) in the world, for multiple editions. Tantalus isn't alone with Riesling in that region, however. Sperling is effectively right across the street and with the same clone of Riesling from the same source planted within days of the Tantalus site in the late 1970s (as local legend has it). The View Winery, next door to Sperling and slightly higher up the slope, also has Riesling. So does SpearHead and Priest Creek farther up the hill from both of them. Farther south, stalwarts Summerhill and CedarCreek both feature Riesling, and Martin's Lane has built a prestigious line based on it. Kelowna is fast becoming Riesling country.

Sipster's Flight Plan: Choose a selection of Rieslings from the same vintage from each winery in Kelowna. For extra fun, add a high-quality German or Australian Riesling to the flight. Also note that Rieslings make for fantastic vertical tasting experiences. Save up the same wine from different vintages for as long as you can and open them all with your friends and fellow sipsters.

PINOT GRIS

The darling of BC white wines has some detractors, but there is certainly no doubting its continued popularity. It supplanted Chardonnay as the most popular white wine at the end of the aughts and hasn't really been ousted from its pedestal since. Pinot Gris can be a lot of things to a lot of people, and it's this diversity of styles that helps with its wide appeal, even if it can make it somewhat unpredictable from producer to producer. Is it going to be super-spicy or floral? Will it be light and crisp like an Italian Pinot Grigio or fuller and richer like an Alsatian Pinot Gris? Only tasting will answer those questions for you.

Pinot Gris stands out in many different regions throughout the Okanagan, but its unpredictability with styles makes it hard to pin down to one in particular. Certainly Naramata has been a big proponent of Pinot Gris over the years and some of those show a spicy floral character that is immensely appealing. In Oliver and Golden Mile, the style is a little more rounded out without losing any of the light spice that lovers of this wine in BC look for.

Sipster's Flight Plan: Try to find as many different styles of Pinot Gris and taste them all, starting with the least acidic. Include a Pinot Gris of a similar quality from Oregon and/or Alsace as well.

CHARDONNAY (OKANAGAN FALLS, OLIVER)

Even with all of the bad PR from the over-oaked monsters of yesteryear, Chardonnay is still a special grape in British Columbia. There is a finesse to the Chardonnays produced here.

Chardonnay is a malleable grape variety that responds to many different winemaking techniques. It is also very forgiving when it comes to mistakes or miscalculations. Even a decade ago, Chardonnay was all over the map with winemaking techniques—malolactic fermentation (or not), oak aging (or not), oak fermentation (or not), aging sur lie (or not). Once a style of production became more widely accepted and winemakers started to look for balance and complexity over trying out some new technique, Chardonnay settled down. Unfortunately by the time that happened, Pinot Gris had overtaken it as the most popular grape variety. This has left Chardonnay alone to find itself in peace from producers who are dedicated to producing it with confidence.

Chard is almost everywhere in BC, but there are small clusters of it producing fantastic examples. Okanagan Falls, with Blue Mountain, Meyer Family Vineyards, and Noble Ridge, among others, feature Chardonnay heavily in their portfolios. Oliver-area producers also feature Chardonnay in a riper style, some of which makes it into wines produced in other regions farther north.

Sipster's Flight Plan: Find Chardonnays from the Okanagan Valley and taste them in descending latitude from north to south.

SIEGERREBE (SHUSWAP, KOOTENAYS, VANCOUVER ISLAND, GULF ISLANDS, FRASER VALLEY)

Okay, hear me out on this. Firstly, aromatic grape varieties (except for Riesling) rarely get mentioned as "serious" or "noble" grape varieties. Gewurztraminer, Ehrenfelser, and those other pungent and often slightly sweeter wine styles rarely get the respect that they deserve. While big reds like Cabernet Sauvignon get called "King Cab the colonizer, the conqueror,"* aromatic grapes like Gewurztraminer generally get far more feminine descriptions and metaphors. When writing about Gewurztraminer, Öz Clarke described it as wanting "to please everybody" and likens its flavour profile to a "vast panoply of make-up, especially mascara and rouge."*

Yup. Old-fashioned, gendered wine writing at its best.

I have included the wonderfully aromatic Siegerrebe here because I believe it has the potential to be taken just as seriously as any other grape variety. Siegerrebe seems to grow well in a lot of different places throughout BC, from Vancouver Island to the Kootenays. This means that for the first time, we have a wine that we can use to compare each region using the same grape variety. Comparing Okanagan Syrah to Vancouver Island Cabernet Foch is never going to tell us anything useful. Comparing two wines from different regions made with Siegerrebe can tell us a lot. What will we find out?

Sipster's Flight Plan: Find one Sieggerebe each from as many regions in BC as you can. Include one from outside of BC in the tasting if possible.

PINOT BLANC (OKANAGAN VALLEY)

Oh, Pinot Blah. Oops, I mean Pinot Blanc. Why do you make such special wines in BC that almost everyone ignores?

Here is why I have included it: I have yet to taste a Pinot Blanc from anywhere else in the world that does what it can do in BC. No other version has that ray of Okanagan sunshine that it has when made here. There is something about its flavour, its vibrancy, and its balance of appealing attributes. Is there a particular region that stands out? Not really. But there are particular producers—Lake Breeze, Blue Mountain, Clos du Soleil, and Mission Hill being standouts—that can really coax

*Clarke, Oz and Rand, Margaret. *Grapes and Wine*, p. 47.
*Ibid, p. 103.

this variety to beautiful new heights. I, for one, want to encourage them to keep doing it.

Sipster's Flight Plan: Try at least two Pinot Blancs from BC along with ones from Germany, Alsace, and Washington State.

RED GRAPE VARIETIES

High-quality red wines are a more recent phenomena in the world of BC wine. Based on trends and the few studies done in the 1970s, whites were thought to be the most suitable for BC's climate and northerly latitude. The first vineyards that planted proper vinifera grapes usually opted for white grapes. With time, more knowledge, experience, and careful observation, the quality of red wines has slowly crept up.

SYRAH (OKANAGAN VALLEY SOUTH OF NARAMATA)

As a guest on an American podcast more than ten years ago, I was asked what *the* two best grape varieties were in BC, red and white. For the red, my mind went over the options: Cab Franc does well, and Merlot is planted everywhere. My mind was on those grapes, but what came out of my mouth was Syrah. Both the host and I were momentarily perplexed, but it suddenly made sense. My rationale still essentially holds true.

Even producers that I'm not particularly enamoured with can make a fairly decent Syrah with some depth and reasonable complexity. I think that means a lot for demonstrating the feasibility of a grape variety within a region. The aggregate level for Syrah in the Okanagan and Similkameen is quite high. The ones that really stand out (i.e. the ones that have been included here and in Volume 1) are truly mind-bending wine experiences. BC has started to find a balance between what it wants to be (an Australian Shiraz) and what it can be (not an Australian Shiraz). BC isn't the Northern Rhone Valley either, nor can it be California or even Washington State. It is a unique and equally profound take on a grape variety that was considered impossible to grow here thirty years ago.

Naramata is pretty much the most northerly sub-region where it can grow in the Okanagan. The Similkameen can take it on too and with a slightly different vibe. In that sense, it is not a universal BC wine grape like Siegerrebe or Pinot Noir. But what it can do in the south Okanagan and Similkameen valleys is pretty amazing.

Sipster's Flight Plan: Try at least three Syrahs from three different producers in different regions—Osoyoos, Oliver, Naramata, Similkameen, etc. Include an international example as well.

CABERNET FRANC (SIMILKAMEEN VALLEY, GOLDEN MILE BENCH, OKANAGAN VALLEY)

Put a bottle of Cabernet Sauvignon next to a bottle of Cabernet Franc on a store shelf and the Sauvignon will outsell the Franc ten to one. Anyone buying a bottle of Franc to be adventurous or just to try something new will be disappointed if they are expecting a similarly big, full-bodied wine as Cab Sauv. If that's what your expectations are (as I believe has been the case for a lot of people), then Cab Franc will never live up to them.

Cabernet Franc loses the initial popularity contest hands down, but I argue that in BC it is slowly winning the quality and style competition over its genetic descendant. Cabernet Franc in BC should be a heady mix and delicate balance between fruit, herbal aromas, and tannins. New producers like Echo Bay and Synchromesh are putting Cabernet Franc front and centre while stalwart producers Fairview Cellars and Hester Creek (both on the Golden Mile Bench, isn't that interesting . . .) continue to produce consistent wines using Franc.

Sipster's Flight Plan: This wine is worth the vertical treatment. Aging Cab Francs brings out those non-fruity aromas and flavours, which aren't always obvious when the wine is young but makes Cab Franc so interesting. Try to save at least three vintages and then open them together for a special occasion.

GAMAY (SIMILKAMEEN VALLEY, OKANAGAN VALLEY)

Why isn't there more Gamay grown in BC? The late Steven Spurrier made a similar comment about this in a talk he gave at Okanagan College in 2019: "Okanagan doesn't grow that much Gamay, but should grow more, to make more of this wonderfully silky, supple, spicy red." Hugh Johnson, author of the *World Atlas of Wine*, suggested in his *2020 Pocket Wine Book* that if you are presented with the opportunity to taste Gamay from the Okanagan, you "seize it."

Here we have two of the top voices of their generation in the world of wine offering their thoughts on this grape variety's potential in BC. It may take a little time to see if that has an effect on vineyard plantings, but for now we should encourage the producers who have embraced Gamay like Okanagan Crush Pad, Robin Ridge, and Blue Mountain. The soils of the Similkameen Valley in particular show off Gamay's wilder and non-fruity side a little better than in the Okanagan. What unites BC's Gamays is the spice and texture and that is not to be missed.

Sipster's Flight Plan: Buy and open more Gamay from BC more often. Just, go. Now. Right now.

PINOT NOIR (VANCOUVER ISLAND, OKANAGAN FALLS, KELOWNA, SIMILKAMEEN VALLEY)

Confession time. Before writing the first volume of *Sipster's*, I was not taken by Pinot Noir in BC. There were too many examples of thin, inconsistent, watery wines with only two flavours. Some were even lighter than the rosés on the next shelf. A few sub-regions have dialled it in (Okanagan Falls and Kelowna), but the inconsistencies were far too widespread ever to take a risk on it as a consumer. As a wine judge, I have personally experienced the horror of thirteen glasses of unknown Pinot Noir placed on the table in front of me. Not every region should bother with Pinot Noir.

The regions that can do it, should. Pinot Noir will put Vancouver Island wines on the map in the coming decade.

There is momentum building, particularly in the Cowichan Valley, that is pointing in the direction of Pinot Noir. Soft, velvety, unique, and inspiring wines that are textured very differently from Okanagan or Similkameen examples. There is something very special happening on Vancouver Island and the Gulf Islands right now that is taking Pinot Noir up a level.

Sipster's Flight Plan: This is the only red grape that you can use to taste wines from multiple growing regions in BC. Find examples from each of the regions mentioned above and compare them.

MERLOT (NARAMATA, OKANAGAN VALLEY)

Merlot, like Pinot Gris, is nearly ubiquitous in the Okanagan. My cynical side has always said that it has succeeded because it is the most easily pronounced grape variety on the wine list. Perhaps I shouldn't have been so cynical because there are plenty of amazing versions of this wine being produced in BC and that kind of thing doesn't happen purely by accident. Merlot was one of the first real breakout reds, with winemaker Ann Sperling at CedarCreek making versions that took the BC wine world by storm in the 1990s. Prior to that, Merlot and most vinifera reds were given little hope of growing properly here let alone being used to make great wine. But it has grown and it has thrived, particularly in places like Naramata where it shows a beautiful depth when grown in the siltier soils below Naramata Road.

I would still argue that Merlot does better as a member of a band, such as Meritage or Cabernet Merlot, rather than as a solo artist single varietal wine. It can be the lead singer and front the group for sure, but there is no doubt that it benefits from the contributions of other players.

Sipster's Flight Plan: Build a flight to taste Merlot's influence on the final wine. Find a Cab-dominant blend that includes Merlot, a Merlot-dominant blend, and a single-variety Merlot (make sure it is 100% Merlot—you might have to ask about this). Try to find wines from the same region if possible and feel free to add more wines with different levels of Merlot.

SIPSTER'S TOP CRUS OF BRITISH COLUMBIA

The term *grand cru* or *premiere cru* is a bit contentious in the whole wine-growing world that isn't France. Literally, *cru* means "growth," and it doesn't make that much sense in English, but in the wine industry, it is an important term. For a winery to be given grand or premiere cru status, it needs to make consistent wines that stand out above all of the others, at least in theory. These wineries create wines that people seek out and that other wineries emulate. They are the shining example of what a great wine can be.

These terms are contentious because of how these statuses are achieved. Is there a way to measure the quality of these wines scientifically? No. Can anyone consider any winery to be a high-status grand cru wine? Sure. Since anyone can do it, some wineries have tried to label themselves as a grand or premiere cru by using similar terms in their marketing literature to give the impression of quality.

However, a winery calling themselves a grand cru is like an athlete giving themselves an Olympic gold medal. Cru status has to be earned through years of consistently producing top-quality wines. Status is then given to them by people not affiliated with the winery, and it is usually the result of a consensus. Sometimes wine "experts," journalists, or writers weigh in by producing a list or ranking of the producers in a region. Sometimes they agree, sometimes they don't. It's the debate and discussion that is the fun part, and if a consensus is reached, at least they have something to celebrate.

The fun thing about creating a list of wineries is that anyone can do it! This has been happening for centuries in France, particularly with the wines of Bordeaux. Courtiers, merchants, and wine enthusiasts made their own lists. Thomas Jefferson, the third president of the United States, lived and worked in France prior to becoming president and made lists of the top chateaux when he visited. Later, a list was made for Napoleon III to classify the wineries of the Medoc region of Bordeaux for the Paris Exposition in 1855. According to author David Peppercorn, this list almost accidentally became written into law and became a template for other wine regions to follow and rank their own wineries by status. Sadly, the Bordeaux list has become entrenched and immobile: it has had only one change made to it since 1855. This immobility has made it stable over the long-term but perhaps at the expense of innovation and adaptation to factors such as climate change.

So what makes a grand cru? There are four main qualities that I believe are important for becoming and remaining one.

Consistent and identifiable vineyard source(s) – The vineyard has to be consistently identified as producing quality wine. Ideally, the winery must own the majority of their vineyards and have direct control over the quality of the fruit. I can recall many instances of wineries winning major awards with a vintage and then having subsequent vintages languish unsaleable in obscurity because the winery was unable to duplicate the traits that won them the award. Why was there no consistency? Did they change winemakers? Did the vineyard sources change? For a winery that is truly a grand cru, neither of these should be a factor. A grand cru–level winery has to have consistent and well-managed vineyard sources and any change in personnel should be irrelevant.

This is where it might be handy to draw a distinction between a vineyard and a winery. Vineyards grow grapes but do not necessarily make wine. Sometimes they sell all of their grapes to wineries. Some wineries own their own vineyards and take on the responsibility of managing them. Status can be given to either the producer or the vineyard. In Burgundy, it is the vineyards that have the status. In Bordeaux, it is the producer (the chateaux). At this point in BC, we do not have enough experience or information to rank the vineyard land in the way that Burgundy does, but I believe we have had sufficient time to figure out which producers make wine consistently and at high levels. For a producer to consistently produce wine at a high level, they will need to have vineyard sources that are themselves consistent and of high quality.

Identifiable and consistent vineyard characteristics – The vineyards must themselves demonstrate attributes relating to soil composition, aspect, slope, orientation, etc. that make them unique. Grapes from the best sites will make high-quality and unique wines regardless of the winery producing them. Some might even argue the process should take place with minimal intervention, even in "challenging" years when the weather is less than ideal. This is the basis of *terroir*, something that is often debated in the wine industry but frequently used in wine marketing. If a particular variety of grapes is being grown on a particular vineyard site, will it make the best wine? Or would it be best with another variety or mix of varieties? The term *terroir* itself is a bit nebulous, which makes debating it all the more difficult because everyone has their own definition of it.

History of consistent high quality – This will have to be relative of course, since the BC wine industry is young at this stage of the game. The wines must show a uniqueness that is clearly evident across multiple vintages. Though the wines in the portfolios don't have to all be long-lived wines, the perception of ageability as a mark of quality cannot be ignored for certain styles of wines like Meritage, Riesling, Pinot Noir, or Chardonnay.

Focused wine portfolio – This is probably the most contentious issue (outside of the concept of terroir itself) because BC has so many wineries that continue to produce a scattershot of wine varieties without any focus. Name one famous wine-growing region where the wineries are all known to produce more than a dozen different varieties of wine and are recognized for all of them equally worldwide? That's right, there aren't any. No winery is ever going to make this list by simply making more different varieties of wines better than the next winery and hoping that something sticks. There are some fabulous wines out there made by wineries with massive and diverse portfolios. For this list I am interested only in wineries that intend on creating the best wine that they can and are focused on that aspect almost single-mindedly on a small portfolio. I don't believe that can be done by growing twenty-five different grape varieties and making thirty different wines from them.

All of the wineries listed here need to have demonstrated consistency with all four of these elements to be considered a premier cru. Note that I have left out the status of grand cru. There is still room to grow so maybe in a future volume of *Sipster's*, one of these wineries will have become distinguished enough for that status.

This is my list of the top cru wineries of the Okanagan and Similkameen Valleys, listed from north to south in their respective Vinters Quality Assurance (VQA) regions with their sub-Geographical Indicators (sub-GIs) in brackets.

THE PREMIER CRUS OF BC

OKANAGAN VALLEY

Tantalus Vineyards (VQA South Kelowna Slopes)
Marichel Vineyards (VQA Naramata)
Terravista Vineyards (VQA Naramata)
Painted Rock Estate Winery (VQA Skaha Bench)
Meyer Family Vineyards (VQA Okanagan Falls)
Blue Mountain Vineyards (VQA Okanagan Falls)
Fairview Cellars (VQA Golden Mile Bench)
Black Hills Estate Winery

SIMILKAMEEN VALLEY

Clos du Soleil
Robin Ridge
Orofino Vineyards
Seven Stones

Where are the other regions like Vancouver Island? Good question. The Okanagan and Similkameen valleys have had a longer history of producing wines on that quality level that other regions have not yet had. In order to satisfy the consistency-over-time factors in the criteria outlined above, wineries have to exist for longer than a decade, which is not yet possible for newer regions or places like Vancouver Island that have traditionally had a high turnover rate for wineries. Clearly, it is only a matter of time. Below is a list of wineries to watch in the coming years. You may already be aware of them since many have appeared in the pages of this guide and in Volume I. They are on my radar and should be on yours as well.

OKANAGAN VALLEY

50th Parallel
Checkmate
Lightning Rock
Martin's Lane
Maverick Estate Winery

SIMILKAMEEN VALLEY

Corcelettes
Vanessa Vineyards

KOOTENAYS

Baillie-Grohman
Valley of the Springs

VANCOUVER ISLAND

Averill Creek
Alderlea Vineyards
Blue Grouse
Emandare Vineyards
Rathjen Cellars
Unsworth

Certainly there are some big names that could have appeared on the list but who have a large and unfocused portfolio of wines. In maintaining a profitable winery within a market based on tourism, the difficulty is building a portfolio of interesting wines to keep people coming through the wine-shop doors. I understand that wineries want to keep wine lovers happy by producing a lot of different wines, but I believe those that choose to focus and master the terroir will ultimately rise to the top of these lists in the future.

Don't agree with me? Make your own list and share it with friends. More involvement is always a good thing.

ACKNOWLEDGEMENTS

A huge thank you to everyone at TouchWood for taking a chance on a very non-traditional book about wine and being so easy to work with on this second volume.

Thank you to all of the wineries who contributed their wines to this new volume.

Thank you to Avery, Paul, Kristi, Jaclyn, and Greg for helping out with tastings (whether they knew it or not at the time).

INDEX